Borders
The basics & beyond

by Jill Reber

Landauer Publishing

Borders
The basics & beyond
by Jill Reber

Copyright © 2009 by Landauer Corporation
Quilt designs copyright © 2008 by Jill Reber

This book was designed, produced, and published by Landauer Books
A division of Landauer Corporation
3100 NW 101st Street, Urbandale, IA 50322
800-557-2144; www.landauercorp.com

President/Publisher: Jeramy Lanigan Landauer
Director of Sales and Operations: Kitty Jacobson
Managing Editor: Jeri Simon
Art Director: Laurel Albright
Technical Editor: Rhonda Matus
Photography: Sue Voegtlin

Library of Congress Control Number: 2008937242

This book is printed on acid-free paper.
Printed in China
10 9 8 7 6 5 4 3 2 1

ISBN 13: 978-0-9800688-9-4
ISBN 10: 0-9800688-9-4

On the front cover: Upper left, Rainbow Mountain Quilt; upper right, Tea and Honey Border
Sampler Quilt; lower left, A Walk in the Woods Border Sampler Quilt; and lower right, Bright &
Batiks Border Sampler Quilt.

4

where to find it

Introduction

Some of my earliest and fondest memories are of being five or six and sitting at my mom's Featherweight sewing machine. I began by making doll clothes and sewing scraps together for doll blankies.

I have been an official quilter since 1976 when I took my first quilting class at age 16. The bicentennial year was a time of a huge quilting resurgence. This helped to move the quilting industry forward as we know it today.

Good quilting basics and skills were stressed in that first class. Although we had yet to see a rotary cutter or quilter's ruler, drafting skills and accuracy of piecing became essentials in my quilt making path.

To help achieve accuracy, my husband and I designed, manufactured, and marketed the Master Piece Cutting System, rotary ruler with slots and Static Stickers that when applied to a ruler, helps you align and cut your fabrics.

This opportunity brought me to my passion and a plethora of quilt designs. Through many years as a quilt designer I have learned that a good quilt design must have three things:

- Basic design elements
- Good color and value contrast
- Correct math applications

These three things will ensure a square and flat quilt top. They can help the whole quilting process and assist you in understanding how to get to the finish line.

Work through this book and allow yourself to bring several of these elements into your next quilt. Think beyond your comfort zone. Try something new, you won't be sorry.

I hope you will enjoy this book and have fun making quilts of your own design.

To the basics and beyond!

Jill Reber

borders—the basics & beyond

Read through the following pages for a quick overview of how to use this book. You'll learn the basics of creating a border sampler quilt and be inspired to go beyond and design your own unique border projects.

getting started—basics and beyond

Borders do more than add to the size of your quilt top; they frame the center and draw the viewer's eye around and back to the focal area of your quilt.

In the following chapters, I have given you the basics of borders, dozens of border options, as well as five block centers to frame and seven additional projects. By following the step-by-step instructions you'll learn tips and tricks to help you choose and design the perfect border for your newest masterpiece. *Jill*

Tools & Equipment offers insight into the basic tools I use when quilting. Most of the equipment and supplies will be familiar to experienced quilters, but it's always fun to experiment with a new ruler, template, or thread.

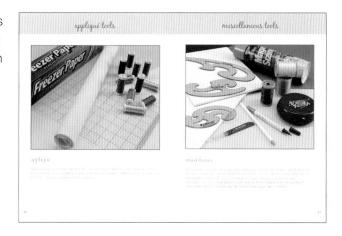

Borders Step-By-Step is filled with information ranging from the basic top-and-bottom wrap border to appliquéing vines and flowers. Pieced blocks, such as Flying Geese and Nine-Patch, highlight the 2", 4", and 6" border options. Instructions for more than 20 borders are provided, so you can pick and choose your favorites and add them to your center block.

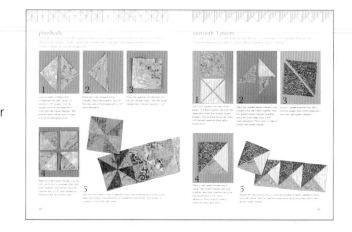

Building A Border Sampler guides you through the process of creating a border sampler quilt. You begin with a 12" center block and add borders in a specific size sequence to finish a beautiful 56" quilt.

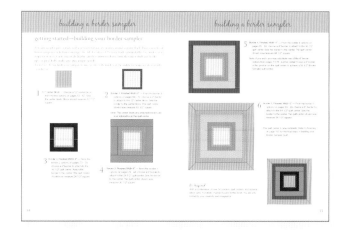

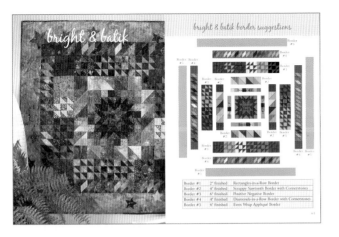

Border Suggestions breaks down the sampler quilts to highlight the borders used in each one.

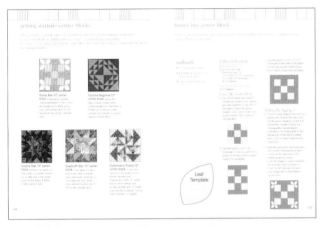

Center Blocks is a group of 12" blocks used to build the border sampler projects. Choose from five center blocks, add borders in different sizes, and soon you will have completed a border sampler quilt.

Projects showcases six table runners and a gorgeous quilt using the border applications taught in the previous chapters. Use your favorite pieced or appliquéd border block to create a completely new design.

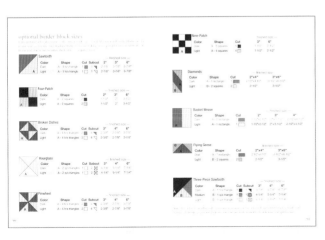

Block size charts provide optional block sizes that allow you to substitute like-size borders. For example, a four-patch block is listed in the border #2—4" border section, but you want to use a pinwheel block border in its place. Turn to the block charts on pages 90 - 91 and find measurements to make 4" pinwheel blocks. Be sure to follow the border size sequence when adding borders to the sampler quilts.

All the options given can be divided into 12" to work with the center block.

tools & supplies

general instructions

getting started

Borders can add a huge impact to a finished quilt. It is best to start with a plan and the proper tools. On the following pages, I have suggested some of the tools that I use every day when sewing. There is no right or wrong, just choose your favorites and get started.

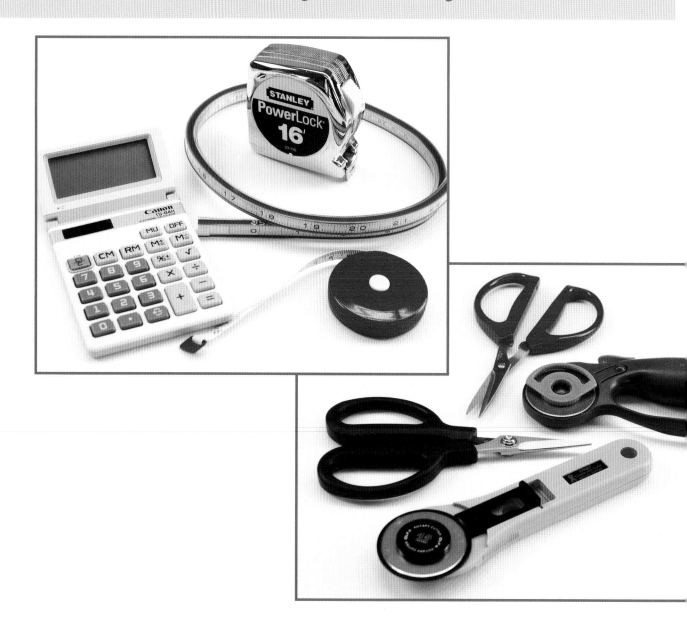

do your math before you cut

Measuring tools are essential when determining the correct size to cut your border strips. A calculator is useful when making a mitered border fit your quilt center. There are several types of measuring tapes available, choose one that works for you.

Cutting mats and tools are another must-have for quilting. Rotary cutters are available with different size blades; choose the one you are most comfortable using. Keep a variety of sharp scissors on hand to clip threads and for cutting appliqué pieces.

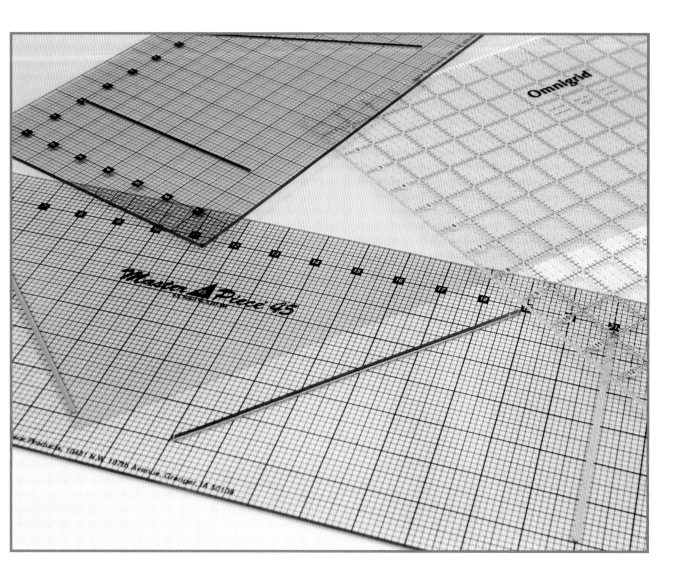

get it straight

A straight cut is important to insuring your border won't wave. Invest in rulers with clear markings and a variety of widths and lengths. Some rulers, such as the Master Piece Quilting rulers above, have slots pre-cut into the acrylic to assist with cutting diamonds and triangles.

appliqué

Appliquéing requires a few tools specific to the technique. Template plastic and freezer paper are used for tracing the design onto the fusible web. Specialty threads, which come in a rainbow of colors, are needed to match the appliqué pieces being stitched to the border.

must-haves

Marking tools, pins, utility thread, and a seam ripper are all necessary tools to have on hand when sewing. Graph paper is also an important tool when charting and planning your designs. Of course, you will need a sewing machine with an accurate 1/4" seam allowance and a walking foot. An ironing board and iron with a good steam feature are essential when pressing the quilt seams.

Some quilters like to use a light spray starch when piecing. If you are planning on making scalloped or curved borders, invest in a curved edge ruler or use household paper plates and bowls.

basic corners

Cornerstones should reflect an element from the quilt center. Repeat a pieced or appliquéd block in the corner or simply choose a favorite color or fabric pattern used in the quilt to anchor your border. You'll find suggestions below, but experiment to determine the corner option that will give your border the biggest impact.

Adding Cornerstones

1. Measure side to side through the middle of the quilt center to calculate the length of the top and bottom border strips. Cut two border strips this size.

2. Measure top to bottom through the middle of the quilt center to determine the length of the side border strips without cornerstones. Cut two borders strips this size.

3. Sew the border strips from Step 1 to the top and bottom of the quilt center using 1/4" seam allowance. Press toward the border strips.

4. Sew a cornerstone to each end of the side border strips from Step 2.

5. Sew the two side border strips to the sides of the quilt center using 1/4" seam allowance. Press toward the border strips.

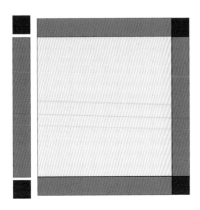

Cornerstone Options

Repeat a pieced block
from the quilt center.

Reduce the size of a favorite
block to use as the cornerstone.

Repeat colors
from the quilt center.

Appliqué the cornerstone with a
design that reflects the quilt center.

Corner Options

Not all quilts need to have 90-degree corners. The table runners beginning on page 114 are an example of other corner shapes.

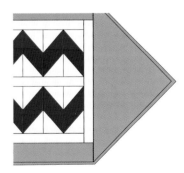

A rounded corner softens the
edge and overall look of a quilt.

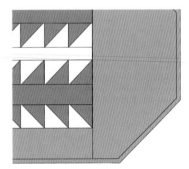

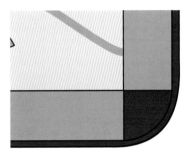

An angled border is a good choice when the border fabric is a continuous design, such as stripes or a large scale pattern.

basic machine or hand appliqué

Appliqué shapes may be stitched to a border or cornerstone by hand or machine. Choose the desired technique and follow the steps below.

Machine Appliqué

1 Following manufacturer's instructions, trace the appliqué shape onto a piece of paper-backed fusible web. Cut the fusible web at least 1/8" from the outside traced line. Fuse the shape to the wrong side of the fabric using a dry iron.

2 Cut out the shape on the drawn line. Peel off the paper backing.

3 Position the appliqué shape on the fabric and fuse.

4 Machine stitch in place.

Hand Appliqué

1 Trace the desired appliqué shape onto template plastic and cut out. Place the template on the right side of the fabric and trace using a pencil, chalk marker, or washable marking tool.

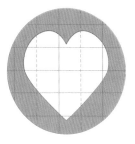

2 Trim fabric 1/4" beyond the traced line. Clip any inside corners.

3 Baste or pin the appliqué shape to the background fabric.

4 Using a thread that matches the fabric, and a slip stitch, needleturn the appliqué in place.

17

basic borders

The best way to work out your border design is to start with a plan. Will you be adding appliqués to the border? Are you using a solid, large print, or directional fabric? What size do you want the quilt to finish? Once you have a plan it allows you to showcase the quilt center and make it stand out.
On the following pages, I have given you instructions for some basic borders that work well with any quilt center. These borders may be used in combination with the pieced and appliquéd borders presented in later chapters.

top-and-bottom-wrap border

A top-and-bottom-wrap border can be used with any fabric and works well with all quilt centers. It also uses less fabric than other borders.

1. Measure side to side through the middle of the quilt center to calculate the length of the top and bottom border strips. Cut two border strips this size.

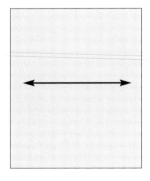

2. Sew the border strips to the top and bottom of the quilt center using 1/4" seam allowance. Press toward the border strips.

3. Measure top to bottom through the middle of the quilt center to determine the length of the side border strips. Cut two borders strips this size. Be sure to include the top and bottom borders when measuring.

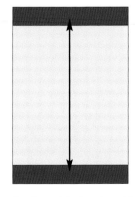

4. Sew the two side border strips to the sides of the quilt center using 1/4" seam allowance. Press toward the border strips.

Note: *If you prefer, the side borders may be added before the top and bottom borders (as shown in the illustration above). You will need to begin by measuring top to bottom through your quilt center and then side to side.*

basic borders

even wrap border

All sides are wrapped in the same direction on an even wrap border. A partial seam is required on the first side. This border style is perfect when using directional fabrics.

1. Measure side to side through the middle of the quilt center. Take this measurement and add the **width** of the border strip. This is the length needed for the border strips.

2. Cut four border strips using the measurement calculated in Step 1.

3. Sew one border strip to the top of the quilt center using a partial seam and 1/4" seam allowance. Press toward the border strip.

4. Continue adding the border strips to the quilt center, as shown. Press seams toward the border strips.

5. Sew the final border to the quilt center and press. Finish sewing the partial seam to connect the borders.

log cabin wrap border

A log cabin wrap border is a good opportunity to repeat fabrics from the quilt center. Different fabrics can be used in each border strip or choose one color palette.

1. Measure side to side through the middle of the quilt center to calculate the length of the top border strip. Cut one border strip this size and sew to the top edge of the quilt. Press toward the border.

2. Measure top to bottom through the middle of the quilt center to determine the length of one side border strip. Be sure to include the top border when measuring. Cut one border strip this size and sew to the side of the quilt. Press toward the border.

3. Measure side to side through the middle of the quilt center to calculate the length of the bottom border strip. Be sure to include the side border when measuring. Cut one border strip this size and sew to the bottom edge of the quilt. Press toward the border.

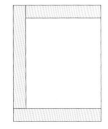

4. Measure top to bottom through the middle of the quilt center to determine the length of the final side border strip. Be sure to include the top and bottom border when measuring. Cut one border strip this size and sew to the side of the quilt. Press toward the border.

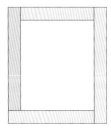

basic mitered borders

A mitered border provides the perfect background for appliqués. It also works well with a lengthwise cut of fabric or a large scale print.

Determining the Border Size

1. Measure the width and length of your quilt. This measurement has seam allowances within, so record both with seam allowances and finished size using the formula below. Do this for both the length and the. width

- Quilt Width with seam allowance =

- Quilt Width finished size minus 1/2" =

- Quilt Length with seam allowance =

- Quilt Length finished size minus 1/2" =

- Finished size of the desired mitered border =

2. Using the measurements determined above, cut two border strips the finished size of the measured **width** of the quilt, plus twice the finished border size. Add 5" for cushion.

3. Using the measurements determined above, cut two border strips the finished size of the measured **length** of the quilt, plus twice the finished border size. Add 5" for cushion.

Adding the Border

1. Mark 1/4" from each end of the border strips using pins or a marking tool.

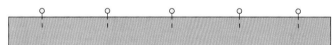

2. Fold the border strips in half lengthwise to find the centers. Mark with a pin or marking tool.

3. Measure half the finished size measurement on each side of the center marked point. Fold in half between center and outer marked point. Mark with a pin or marking tool.

4. Mark 1/4" on each corner of the quilt center using a pin or marking tool.

5. Fold the quilt center in half and mark the center of each side with a pin or marking tool.

6. Fold the quilt center in half again from the marked center point to the edge of the quilt top. Mark the center point with a pin or marking tool.

Note: *You should now have five marked points to match and align the border on your quilt center.*

7. Pin the borders to the quilt center matching the marked points.

8. Beginning and ending at the corner with the marked 1/4" point, backstitch and sew the border strip to the quilt center.

9. Repeat for the remaining borders.

10. Press the seam towards the border.

Mitering the Corners

1. Working on the ironing board, lay one border vertically on the board.

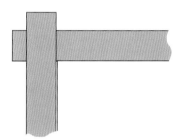

2. Bring the adjoining border up and fold at a 45-degree angle. It should lay on top of the border in Step 1. Press.

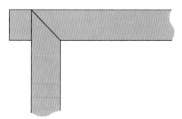

3. Fold the quilt center on the diagonal, right sides together.

4. The pressed border should now be laying flat on top of the other border strip. Pin along creased line.

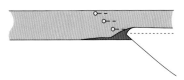

5. Stitch on the creased line, backstitching 1/4" from the edges. Trim seam to 1/4". Press.

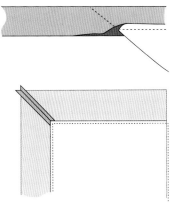

6. Repeat for remaining corners.

Binding

The final step in finishing a quilt is attaching the binding. Below are the steps to finish your quilt with one of the most common binding styles, a French-fold binding with mitered corners.

1. Sew the short ends of the binding strips, right sides together, with diagonal seams. Trim 1/4" from sewn line and press open. Fold the binding strips, wrong sides together, in half lengthwise, and press.

2. Fold under a 1/2" hem at the beginning of the binding. Leaving approximately 4" of binding free, begin sewing the binding to the front of the quilt sandwich at the center on the bottom edge. Use a 1/4" seam allowance. Sew 1/4" from the first corner, stop, and clip the threads. Remove the quilt sandwich from under the presser foot.

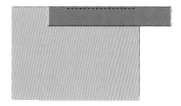

3. Fold the binding strip up at a 45-degree angle, as shown.

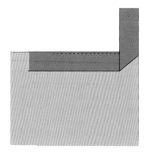

4. Fold the binding strip back down upon itself, making sure that the horizontal fold in the binding is even with the top edge of the quilt sandwich, as shown. Begin sewing the binding to the quilt exactly where the previous seam ended. Continue sewing and repeat Steps 2 and 3 at each remaining corner.

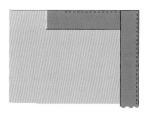

5. To end, slide the end of the binding into the free portion at the beginning; sew the remaining seam.

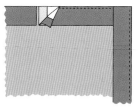

6. Bring the binding over the edge to the backing side of the quilt sandwich, and hand stitch in place. A folded miter will form at each corner; stitch these folds closed.

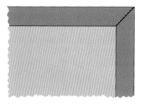

border vocabulary

Appliqué Border—A border with fabric shapes or motifs sewn onto it for extra dimension or interest.

Batting—The thin, soft middle layer that is between the backing and front of the quilt.

Bias Strips—Narrow strips of fabric cut on the bias grain. Bias is used to form shapes, such as vines and stems in an appliqué border. Wider strips can be used for binding.

Binding—The fabric used to cover the raw edges of the top, bottom, and batting layers of a quilt. It is also the technique of finishing the edges of a quilt.

Blocks—The units sewn together to make up a quilt center or border.

Center Block—The pieced or appliquéd block in the middle of a quilt top. All other elements of the quilt are built around this block.

Cornerstones—A block added to the end of a border strip.

Fat-eighth—A 9" x 22" piece of fabric.

Fat-quarter—A 18" x 22" piece of fabric.

Hand Appliqué—Method of sewing fabric shapes onto a fabric background by hand.

Machine Appliqué—Method of sewing fabric shapes onto a fabric background with a sewing machine.

Mitering—Sewing a 45-degree angle to join borders or binding at corners.

Pieced Border—A border consisting of pieced blocks or units.

Piecing—The process of sewing fabric pieces together to create a block or quilt top.

Pressing—Using an iron to crease or fold fabric. When pressing, raise the iron up and down. Avoid sliding it back and forth.

Quarter-square Triangles—A square cut diagonally twice to create quarter-square triangles.

Quilt Border—Borders frame the center of a quilt and give it a finished look. Borders may be pieced, appliqué, or plain fabric.

Quilt Center—The pieced or appliquéd setting of a quilt top. The quilt center includes the center block and borders.

Quilt Sandwich—The three layers of a quilt, which include the top, batting, and backing.

Sashing—Strips of fabric used to separate blocks in a quilt top.

Seam Allowance—The distance between the raw edge and the seam line.

Templates—A shape or pattern piece for piecing or appliqué.

Triangle-squares—A square cut in half diagonally to create two half-square triangles.

Whole Fabric Border—A border style using one fabric. This style is used in a top-and-bottom wrap, even wrap, log cabin wrap, or mitered border.

delectable
mountain

rectangles–
in-a-row

broken dishes
pinwheels
basket weave

maple leaf
flying geese

squares-in-a-row
scrappy sawtooth

positive
negative

diamonds–
in-a-row

borders
step-by-step

The border around a quilt is much like the frame around a piece of art. It draws and keeps the eye of the viewer at the center of your masterpiece.

You'll find step-by-step instructions for over a dozen simple border blocks that combine to add drama and style to any quilt.

four-patch

Four-patch border blocks are quick and easy to sew. Repeat fabrics from the quilt center or choose complementary colors to create the four-patch blocks.

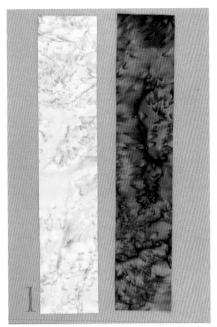

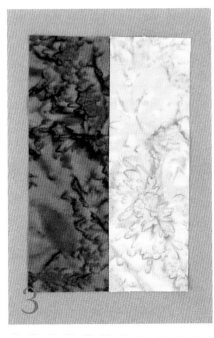

Cut two 2-1/2" fabric strips in complementary colors.
The fabric strips above will make a 4" finished four-patch border block. Choose any size you desire to frame your quilt center.

Place the strips right sides together and sew with a 1/4" seam to create one strip set.

Press seam allowance to one side.

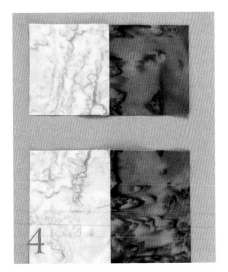

Cut the strip set into 2-1/2" segments.

Place two 2-1/2" segments right sides together. Be sure to place the dark square of one segment on top of the light square of the second segment. Sew together with a 1/4" seam allowance and press. The four-patch unit should measure 4-1/2".

scrappy four-patch

Use a variety of fabrics to create a more scrappy look in your quilt border. Pull colors of varying shades from the quilt center to use in a scrappy four-patch border.

1

The scrappy four-patch border squares above are 2-1/2". These squares can be sized to create a wider or more narrow border. Cut four 2-1/2" squares in a variety of colors.

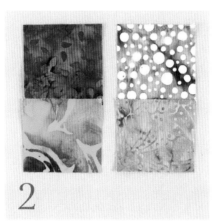

2

Sew the squares together in sets of two and press the seam allowances.

3

Sew the segments together in random order to create a scrappy four-patch unit.

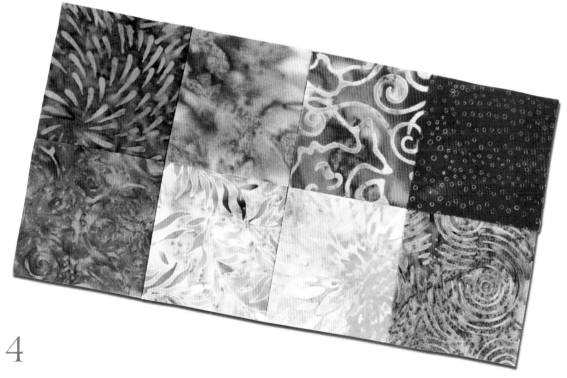

4

Join the number of scrappy four-patch units needed to frame the quilt center.

nine-patch checkerboard

A nine-patch checkerboard border serves to create a transition between a lighter quilt center and a dark border.

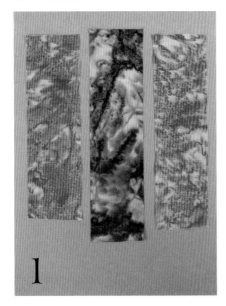

1 Cut two light 2-1/2" fabric strips and one dark 2-1/2" fabric strip.
The fabric strips above will make a 6" finished nine-patch checkerboard border block. Adjust the width of the strips to create the border size you need.

2 Cut two dark 2-1/2" fabric strips and one light 2-1/2" fabric strip.

3 Sew the fabric strips together with a 1/4" seam to make one dark/light/dark strip set.

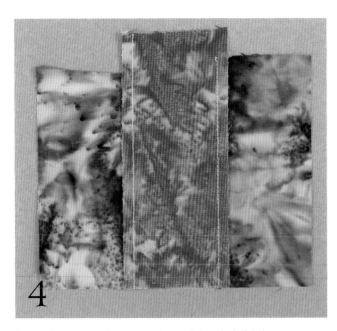
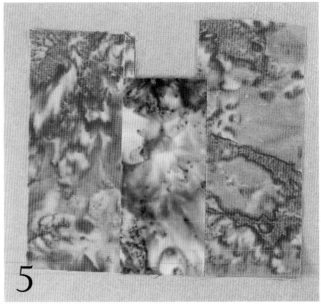

4 Press the seam allowances toward the dark fabric.

5 Following the instructions in step 3 make one light/dark/light strip set. Press.

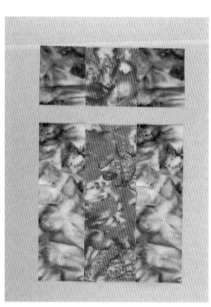

Cut each strip set into
2-1/2" segments.

6

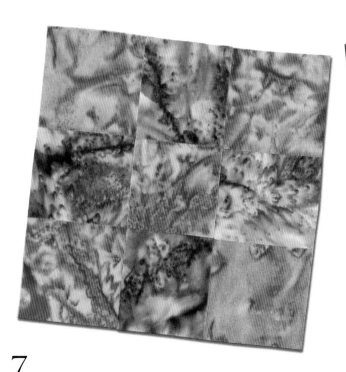

7

Place a 2-1/2" light/dark/light segment, right sides together, on a 2-1/2" dark/light/dark segment. Match the seam lines and sew together with a 1/4" seam allowance. Press. Place a 2-1/2" light/dark/light segment on top of the unit just sewn, right sides together. Match the seam lines and be sure the light and dark squares are creating a checkerboard pattern. Sew together to create a nine-patch checkerboard block. Press. Repeat using two dark/light/dark and one light/dark/light 2-1/2" segments.

squares-in-a-row

Squares-in-a-row is a simple way to frame any quilt center. Squares can be arranged in a repeating order for a formal look or placed randomly, as demonstrated below, for a more casual feel.

Cut assorted fabric squares all one size. You may also choose to use only one or two fabrics.

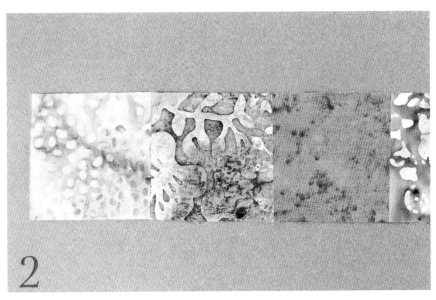

2

Sew squares together in random order using a 1/4" seam allowance. Press seams in one direction.

3

Continue sewing squares together until the strip is the desired length of your border.

rectangles-in-a-row

Rectangles are the perfect way to increase the size of a quilt center since they can be cut any length and still add a punch.

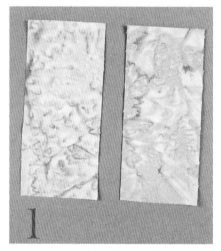

Determine the desired size of the quilt border. Cut rectangles the chosen size in a variety of colors. The rectangles in the sample are 2-1/2" x 6-1/2".

Place two rectangles together, right sides facing. Sew a 1/4" seam along the long side of the rectangle. Press seam to one side. Continue adding rectangles to the unit until border is the desired length. Press all seams in one direction.

3

Repeat the steps above until you have the number of borders needed for your quilt center.

basket weave

A basket weave border creates an illusion of woven fabric. It is easy to accomplish by alternating the direction of pairs of rectangles.

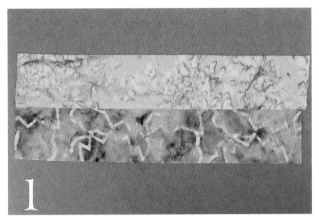

Cut a variety of 2-1/2" strips. Sew these strips together in groups of two using a 1/4" seam allowance. Press seams in one direction. Use fabrics from the quilt center or choose ones that complement the overall hue of the quilt. The example given will make 4"x4" finished segments.

Cut the completed strip sets into 4-1/2" segments.

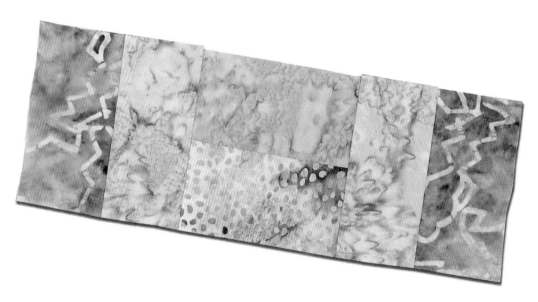

Sew the 4-1/2" segments together alternating the direction of each segment, as shown above. Press seams in one direction. Continue adding segments until the strip is the correct length for your border.

scrappy sawtooth

Borders with triangles, like the scrappy saw tooth, are a great way to use fabric scraps. Triangles can be arranged within a border block to create the illusion of movement.

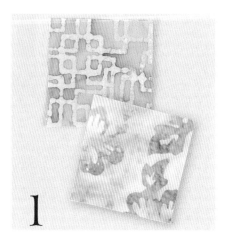

1

Using a variety of fabrics that complement the quilt center, cut several 2-7/8" squares. The example given is for a 2" finished half-square triangle for a scrappy sawtooth border.

2

Cut each square once on the diagonal to form two triangles.

3

Place two complementary color triangles, right sides together. Sew on the long side of the triangles with a 1/4" seam allowance.

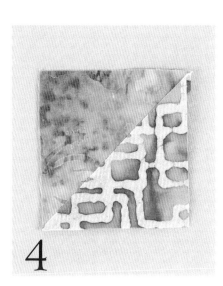

4

Press the seams in one direction and trim the outside edges. The half-square triangle block should measure 2-1/2".

5

Join the half-square triangle blocks to form a scrappy sawtooth border, the size needed for one side of the quilt center. Repeat for all sides of the quilt center.

diamonds-in-a-row

Diamond borders appear difficult to piece, but when broken down into single blocks they are actually easy. They also provide numerous possibilities for adding color and directional movement to a quilt border.

Cut one 2-1/2" by 4-1/2" rectangle from a dark fabric. Cut two 2-1/2" squares from a light fabric. You may choose to reverse the colors of the diamond block for a completely different look. The example shown is for a 2" x 4" finished diamond block.

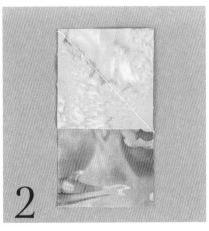

Lay a light square even with one side of the dark rectangle, right sides together. Sew the fabrics together with a diagonal (corner to corner) seam.

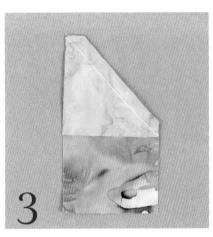

Trim the fabric 1/4" from the sewn line, as shown.

Press the seam allowance in one direction. Press the unit open.

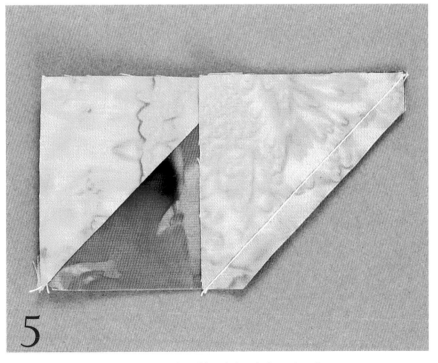

Repeat Steps 2—4 for the opposite side of the dark rectangle.

6 Press seam allowance in one direction. Press the diamond block open. This is a left diamond block. The block should measure 2" x 4".

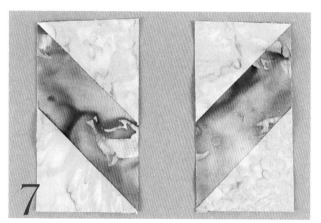

7 To create a right diamond block, shown above at right, place the light square on the corner of the dark rectangle and sew a diagonal line beginning at the upper right hand corner of the square. Trim 1/4" from seam line and press. Repeat with opposite corner of rectangle to complete one block.

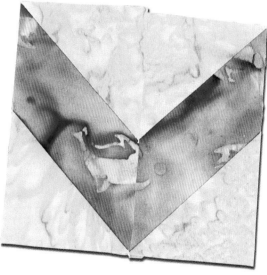

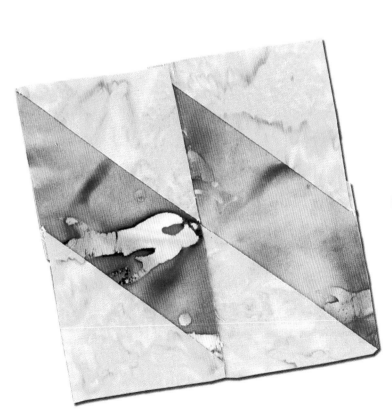

8 Lay out the diamond blocks in a pattern to complement the quilt. The example at left shows left diamond blocks sewn together to create a directional border. The example above shows diamond blocks sewn together to create a zigzag pattern.

scrappy flying geese

Flying geese blocks add a feeling of motion around the edge of a quilt center. It is one of the most versatile border options. A quilter can achieve completely different looks by using a multitude of scrap fabrics or a simple two-color palette.

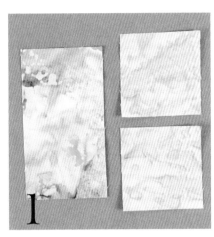

1

Cut one 2-1/2" x 4-1/2" rectangle and two 2-1/2" squares from complementary fabrics. The example above is for a 2" x 4" finished flying geese unit.

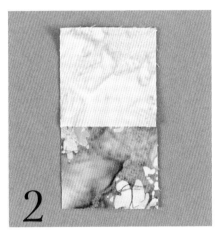

2

Lay one square even with one side of the rectangle, right sides together. Sew the fabrics together with a diagonal (corner to corner) seam.

3

Trim the fabric 1/4" from the sewn line, as shown.

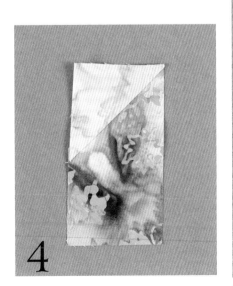

4

Press the unit open.

5

Repeat Steps 2—4 for the opposite side of the rectangle.

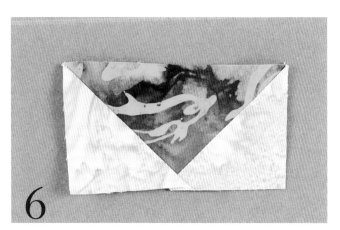

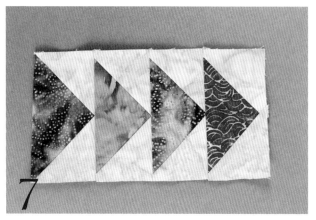

6

Press the finished flying geese unit open. Repeat steps 1—5 to make the needed number of flying geese units.

7

Place two flying geese units together right sides together. Sew a 1/4" seam along one long side of the rectangle. Press seam to one side. Continue adding flying geese units until border is the length needed. Press all seams in one direction. Before sewing, check to make sure your geese are all 'flying' in the same direction.

8

Repeat the steps above until you have the number of borders needed to frame all sides of your quilt center.

pinwheels

Much like a flying geese border, a pinwheel border gives the quilt center an illusion of movement. Color choices in the border also play a part in the overall look of the quilt. The border example below uses a variety of fabrics for a more scrappy feel.

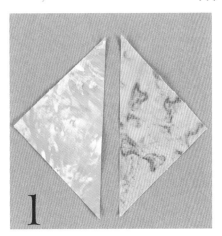

1

Using a variety of fabrics that complement the quilt center, cut several 2-7/8" squares. Cut the squares once on the diagonal to make two half-square triangles. The example given will be used to make a 4" finished pinwheel block.

2

Place two color complementary triangles right sides together. Sew on the long side of the triangle with a 1/4" seam allowance.

3

Press the seams in one direction and trim the outside edges. The half-square triangle block should measure 2-1/2".

4

Make four half-square triangles. Lay the units out to form a pinwheel. With right sides together, sew the two top units together with a 1/4" seam allowance. Repeat for the two bottom units.

5

Sew the rows made in Step 4 together to form one pinwheel block (photo inset). Make the number of pinwheel blocks needed for your border. Join the blocks together to frame the quilt center.

three-piece sawtooth

This variation of the sawtooth block uses two different sizes of triangles. The example below uses three fabrics in complementary colors to create a border that keeps the eye moving.

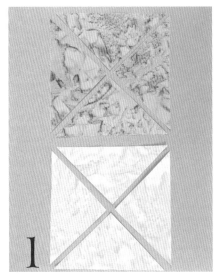

1

Cut 5-1/4" squares from two of the fabrics. Cut these squares twice on the diagonal to make four quarter-square triangles. The example above will make a 4" finished three-piece sawtooth border block.

2

Place two quarter-square triangles, one of each color, right sides together. Sew the quarter-square triangles together along the short edge using a 1/4" seam allowance. Press open to make a pieced half-square triangle.

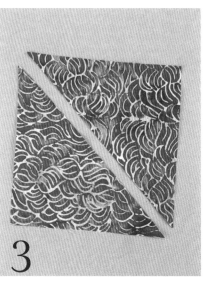

3

Cut a 4-7/8" square from the third fabric. Cut the square once on the diagonal to form two half-square triangles.

4

Place a half-square triangle and a pieced half-square triangle right sides together. Sew them together along the long edge using a 1/4" seam allowance. Press open to make a three-piece sawtooth block.

5

Repeat the steps above until you have the number of blocks needed to frame your quilt center. Sew the three-piece sawtooth blocks into rows until borders are the length needed.

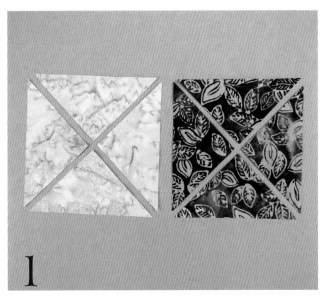

hourglass

The hourglass block is one of the many border options formed with triangles. In the example below one light and one dark fabric was used. To create a more scrappy look use a variety of colors to enhance the quilt center.

Cut 5-1/4" squares from one light and one dark fabric. Cut the squares into quarters diagonally to make four quarter-square triangles. The example above will form a 4" finished hourglass block.

Lay a light triangle on top a dark triangle, right sides together. Sew the triangles together in pairs using a 1/4" seam allowance. Press the triangle units open. Sew the two units together to form an hourglass block. Make the number of hourglass blocks needed to frame the quilt center.

3

Sew the hourglass blocks into rows, alternating the direction of the blocks.

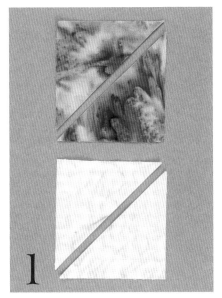

broken dishes

The broken dishes block will give your border added visual interest. Half-square triangles form this simple block that tricks the eye into seeing a set-on-point block. Pull the colors from the center of the quilt for a variety of two color blocks.

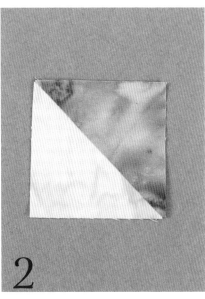

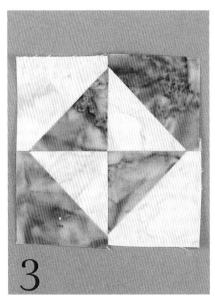

1
Cut 2-7/8" squares from light and dark fabrics. Cut the squares in half diagonally to make two half-square triangles from each square. The example above will form a 4" finished broken dishes block.

2
Lay a light triangle on top a dark triangle, right sides together. Sew the light and dark triangles together in pairs, using a 1/4" seam allowance, to form four triangle squares.

3
Sew the four triangle squares together as shown to make a broken dishes block. Make the number of broken dishes blocks needed for your border.

4
Join the broken dishes blocks into rows until the borders are the length needed.

bias vines

A gently curving vine adds softness and movement to a quilt border. To achieve a curve without puckers, the fabric for vines need to be cut on the bias. Appliquéing flowers or leaves on or around the vine will give the quilt added interest.

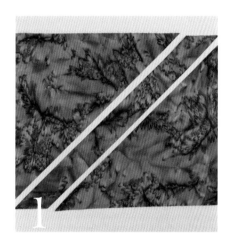
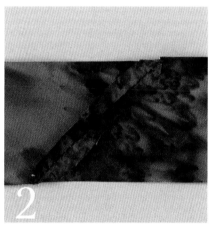
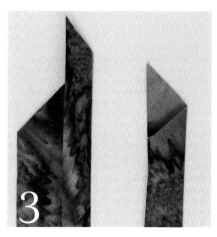

1. Cut a 45-degree angle off one edge of a fabric rectangle. Cut bias strips the width needed for your finished vine. The example above shows 1-1/2" bias strips that will form a 1/2" finished vine.

2. Sew the bias strips together to form one continuous piece. Handle the bias gently to avoid stretching. Press the seams open.

3. Fold and press the bias strip into thirds to form a finished vine.

4. Examples above (left-right) are:
1-1/2" bias strip = 1/2" finished vine
1-3/4" bias strip = 5/8" finished vine
2" bias strip = 3/4" finished vine

5. Position the vine strip on the quilt border in an eye-pleasing manner creating curves where desired. Pin the vine in place. Hand or machine stitch to the border.

stitches

To secure an outside edge of a pieced border it is helpful to "stay" stitch it. Use the stitch examples below to secure the outer edge of your quilt border.

Straight Stitch

Zig Zag Stitch

Serger Stitch

positive negative

Positive negative blocks are formed with two contrasting fabrics. Reverse the lights and darks to achieve a different look.

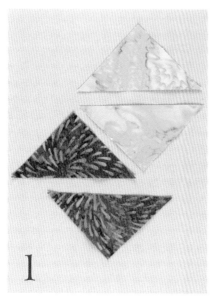

1

To make one positive and one negative block, cut 12, 2-7/8" squares from both the light and dark fabric. Cut the squares in half diagonally to form half-square triangles. Also, cut three 2-1/2" light squares. The example given will make a 6" finished positive block.

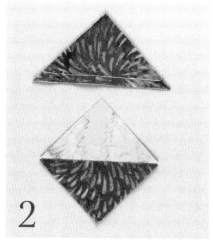

2

Sew the light and dark triangles together in pairs with a 1/4" seam allowance. Press toward the dark fabric. Trim the corners to create a triangle-square. Six triangle-squares are needed for the block.

3

Arrange the squares into rows, as shown, and sew together using a 1/4" seam allowance.

4

Sew the rows together to form a positive block.

5

Reverse the position of the triangle-squares and use three 2-1/2" dark squares to create a negative block. Make the number of blocks needed for the quilt border.

maple leaf

While a maple leaf block may be seen more often in the center of a quilt, it makes a wonderful border. Make a series of blocks in a variety of colors taken from the quilt center.

Cut 2, 2-7/8" squares of a light and dark fabric. Cut the squares in half diagonally to make two triangles from each square. The example given will make a 6" finished maple leaf block.

Sew the light and dark triangles together in pairs with a 1/4" seam allowance. Press toward the dark fabric. Trim the corners to create a triangle-square. Four triangle-squares are needed for the maple leaf block.

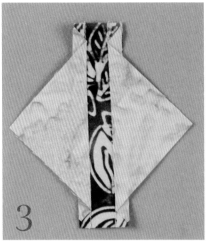

Cut a 2-5/8" square from the light fabric. Cut square on the diagonal to form two triangles. Make a stem square by centering and sewing a triangle on a 1" x 4" dark rectangle. Repeat with another triangle on the opposite edge of the dark rectangle. Press.

Trim the ends of the strip so the stem square measures 2-1/2".

Cut a 2-1/2" light and dark square. Cut a 2-1/2" x 4-1/2" dark rectangle. Arrange the fabric units into rows and sew. Sew rows together to form a maple leaf block.

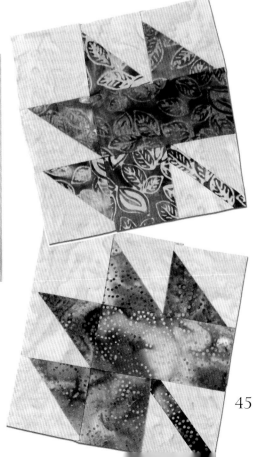

sawtooth star

Sawtooth star blocks provide a great opportunity to implement all the quilt center's colors into the quilt border.

1

Cut 4, 2" x 3-1/2" rectangle and 8, 2" squares from complementary fabrics. The example above will be used to form a 6" finished sawtooth star block.

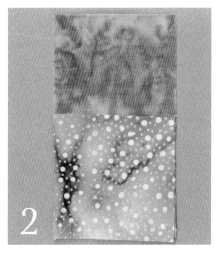

2

Lay one square even with one side of the rectangle, right sides together. Sew the fabrics together with a diagonal (corner to corner) seam. Trim the fabric 1/4" from the sewn line. Press open.

3

Repeat steps 1—2 for the opposite side of the rectangle.

4

Press open to form one flying geese unit. Repeat steps 1—3 to make three additional flying geese units.

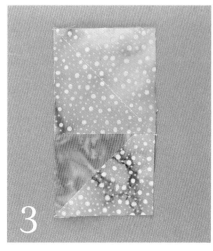

5

Arrange four flying geese units, four 2" squares, and one 3-1/2" square in rows, as shown. Sew units into rows. Sew the rows together to form a sawtooth block.

delectable mountain

Delectable mountain blocks add a touch of drama to any quilt border. Use a two color palette or pull fabrics from your stash to enhance the quilt center.

Cut 3, 2-3/8" squares from a light and dark fabric, 1, 3-7/8" square from the medium fabric, and 1, 6-7/8" square and 1, 2" square from the dark fabric. Cut all the squares in half diagonally, *except the 2" dark square*, to make two triangles from each square. The example given will form a 6" finished delectable mountain block.

Sew the light and dark small triangles together with a 1/4" seam allowance. Press toward the dark fabric. Trim the corners to create a triangle-square.

Arrange the units as shown and sew together to form a delectable mountain block. Repeat to make the number of blocks needed for the quilt border.

mitered corners

Mitered corners are the perfect border application when using large scale prints, stripes, or plaids in your border. It is also a wonderful background when working with an appliqué border.

1

To determine the length of your borders measure the length of your quilt center, plus the width of your border. Multiply the border width total by two and add 5-inches. Cut the side border strips to this size.

Repeat steps for the top and bottom borders, measuring the width of the quilt center plus borders formula.

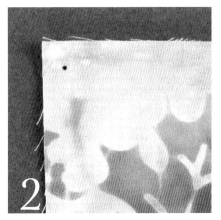

2

Mark the 1/4" seam allowance with a dot at each corner of the quilt center.

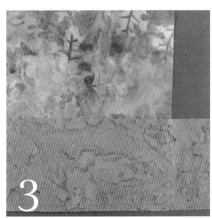

3

Align a border strip with the edge of the quilt center. Extend the strip the width of the border plus 2-1/2" beyond the edge. Sew border strip to quilt center, starting and stopping at the dot. Backstitch to secure.

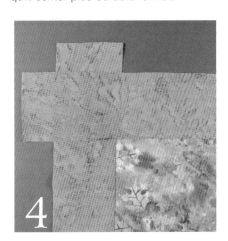

4

Repeat step 3 for remaining border strips. Remember to start and stop at the marked dot and backstitch.

5

Align two borders, one on top of the other. One of the borders should be straight and the other should have a 45-degree fold. Press.

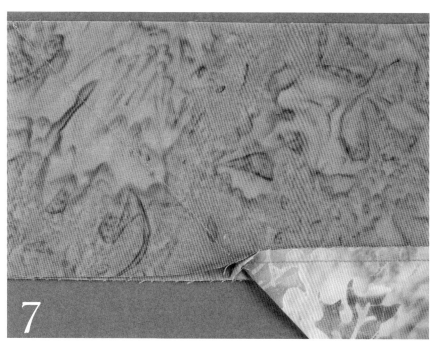

Fold the quilt center on the diagonal, right sides together. Fold the pressed border strip over the flat one, right sides together, aligning outer edges. Place pins over the fold, as shown.

Beginning 1/4" from the inner edge, stitch along the fold. Backstitch at the top and bottom. Trim 1/4" from the stitching line. Press the seam open.

Repeat for each corner of the quilt border.

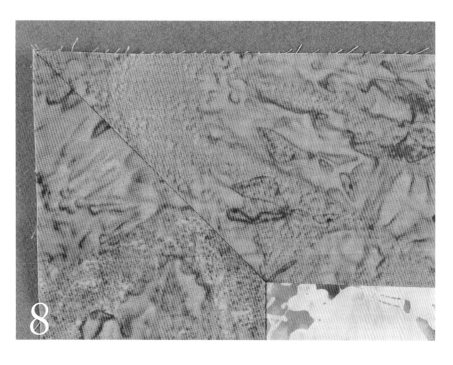

machine appliqué

Appliqués can soften the edges of a quilt center and can be combined with a pieced border or cornerstones. Paper-backed fusible web makes it easy to use appliqués with sharp edges that would be difficult to piece or turn under.

Cut the fusible web at least 1/8" from the outside traced line. Fuse the shape to the wrong side of the fabric using a dry iron.

Following manufacturer's instructions, trace the appliqué shape onto a piece of paper-backed fusible web.

Cut out the shape on the drawn line.

Peel off the paper backing.

Position the appliqué shape on the fabric and fuse. Machine stitch in place.

hand appliqué

Template plastic or freezer paper can be used for hand (needleturn) appliqué. In the example below, the appliqué was cut from template plastic. The appliqué shape is sewn down by hand using your needle to fold the seam allowance under and stitch.

Trace the desired appliqué shape onto template plastic and cut out.

Place the template on the right side of the fabric and trace using a pencil, chalk marker, or washable marking tool.

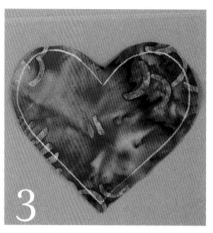

Trim fabric 1/4" beyond the traced line. Clip any inside corners.

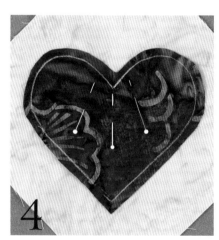

Baste or pin the appliqué shape to the background fabric.

Using a thread that matches the fabric, and a slip stitch, needleturn the appliqué in place.

tea
and
honey

soft
pastels

bright
&
batik

beautiful
batiks

border samplers

Begin by selecting one of the five 12" center blocks. Choose a combination of 2", 4", 6", and appliquéd borders to frame the center block and complete a 56" square finished border sampler quilt. Three border sampler quilts are shown, but I encourage you to pick and choose the center blocks and borders that appeal to you.

getting started—building your border sampler

A border sampler quilt is made with a series of various size borders around a center block. Three examples of border samplers can be found on pages 56 - 61. Each has a 12" center block surrounded by five borders in a sequence of sizes. Create one of the border samplers shown or choose from the center block and border options provided to make your own unique sampler.

Important: As you build your sampler be sure to attach the borders in the width-size sequence shown in the steps below.

1   12" Center Block — Choose a 12" center block from the five options on pages 63 - 67. Sew the center block. Block should measure 12-1/2" square.

2   Border 1; Finished Width 2" — From the border 1 options on pages 69 - 72, choose a 2" border to attach to the 12" center block. Sew the border to the center block. The quilt center should now measure 16-1/2" square.

Note: The center block and attached borders are now referred to as the quilt center.

3   Border 2; Finished Width 4" — From the border 2 options on pages 73 - 78, choose a 4" border to attach to the 16-1/2" quilt center. Attach the border to the center. The quilt center should now measure 24-1/2" square.

4   Border 3; Finished Width 6" — From the border 3 options on pages 79 - 84, choose a 6" border to attach to the 24-1/2" quilt center. Sew the border to the center. The quilt center should now measure 36-1/2" square.

5 Border 4; Finished Width 4" — From the border 4 options on pages 85 - 89, choose a 4" border to attach to the 36-1/2" quilt center. Sew the border to the center. The quilt center should now measure 44-1/2" square.

Note: If you wish, you may substitute one of the 4" border options from pages 73-78. Just be certain to use a 4" border in this position on the quilt center to achieve a 56-1/2" Border Sampler quilt center.

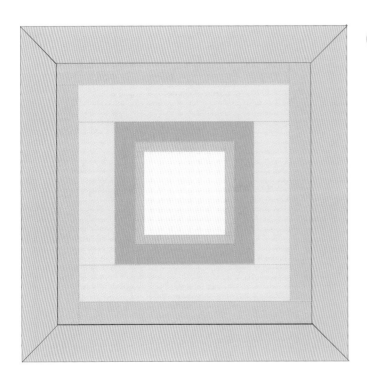

6 Border 5; Finished Width 6" — From the border 5 options on pages 93 - 99, choose a 6" border to attach to the 44-1/2" quilt center. Sew the border to the center. The quilt center should now measure 56-1/2" square.

The quilt center is now complete. Refer to Finishing on page 107 for the final steps in building your Border Sampler Quilt.

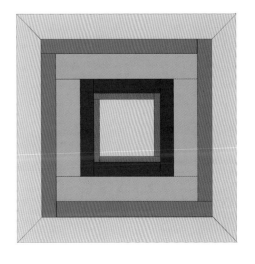

Be Inspired

With a combination of over 50 borders, quilt centers, and optional block sizes, hundreds of projects exist in this book. You are only limited by your creativity and imagination.

tea and honey

tea and honey border suggestions

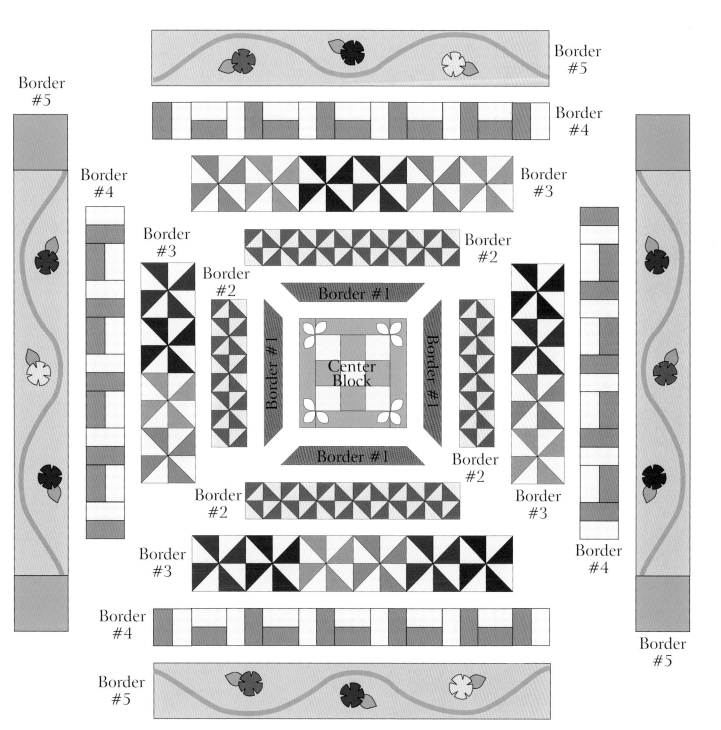

Border #1	2" finished	Mitered Border
Border #2	4" finished	Broken Dishes Border
Border #3	6" finished	Pinwheel Border
Border #4	4" finished	Basket Weave Border
Border #5	6" finished	Cornerstone Appliqué Border

a walk in the woods

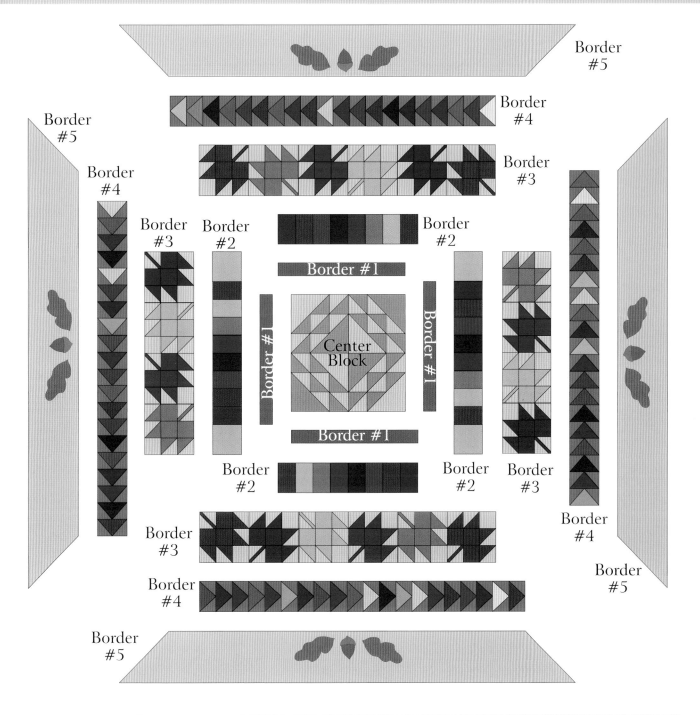

Border #1	2" finished	Even Wrap Border
Border #2	4" finished	Rectangles-in-a-Row with Cornerstones Border
Border #3	6" finished	Maple Leaf Border
Border #4	4" finished	Flying Geese Border
Border #5	6" finished	Mitered Appliqué Border

bright & batik

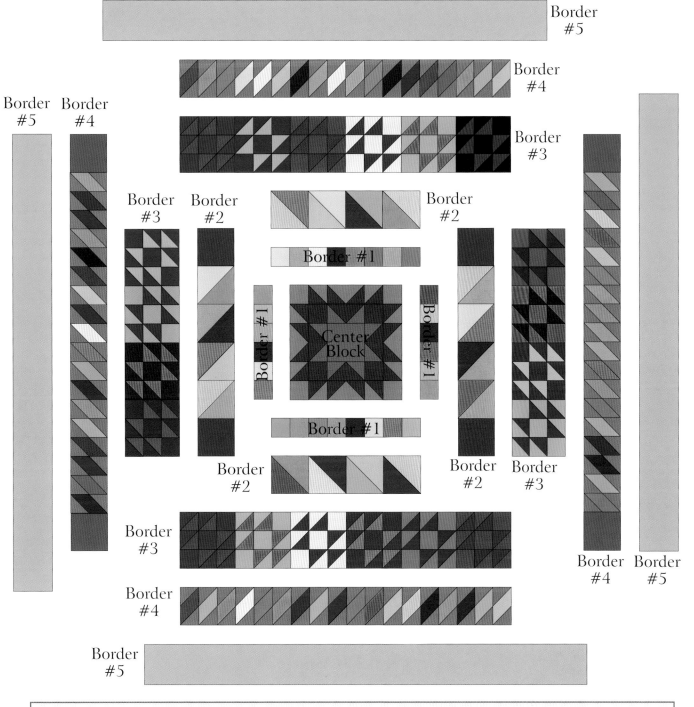

Border #1	2" finished	Rectangles-in-a-Row Border
Border #2	4" finished	Scrappy Sawtooth Border with Cornerstones
Border #3	6" finished	Positive Negative Border
Border #4	4" finished	Diamonds-in-a-Row Border with Cornerstones
Border #5	6" finished	Even Wrap Appliqué Border

getting started—center blocks

A border sampler quilt is the perfect way to showcase a favorite pieced or appliquéd center block.
Five 12" center blocks are highlighted in this chapter, each with its own unique look.
Grab some favorite fabrics and stitch up a center block. Then get ready to enhance your block with pieced
and appliquéd borders.

Honey Bee 12" center block is beautiful in pastels. Leaves appliquéd on the corners encourage you to think spring. This is the center block for the Tea and Honey border sampler quilt.

Walk in the Woods 12" center block shows the high contrast created when combining light and dark fabrics. A Walk in the Woods border sampler quilt features this center block.

Double Star 12" center block stitched in a variety of blue batiks is a breath of fresh air. Double Star is the center block for the Bright & Batik border sampler quilt.

Sawtooth Star 12" center block looks great in brights, but would make a dramatic black and white center block. The Sawtooth Star center block will work well in any of the border sampler quilts.

Dutchman's Puzzle 12" center block is one more option for the center of your border sampler quilt. Choose any of the 12" center blocks here to begin your border sampler quilt. Or create your own block design—just be sure it finishes 12" square.

honey bee center block

The honey bee center block, a nine-patch framed with a top-and-bottom wrap border, is enhanced with appliquéd leaves at the corners.

materials

- 1/6 yard of green fabric
- Fat eighth or 1/8 yard each of two yellow fabrics
- Paper-backed fusible web

Cutting Instructions

From green fabric, cut:
1—2-3/4" x 42" strip.
   From the strip, cut:
   2—2-3/4" x 12-1/2" rectangles.
   2—2-3/4" x 8" rectangles.
   4—3" squares.

From one yellow fabric, cut:
5—3" squares.

Piecing the Center Block

1. Lay out the green and yellow 3" squares as shown in the diagram and sew together in rows. Press the seams toward the green squares. Join rows to make one nine-patch block. Press seams in one direction.

2. Sew the green 2-3/4" x 8" rectangles to the top and bottom edges of the block. Press seams toward the rectangles.

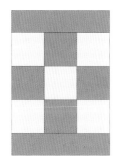

3. Sew the green 2-3/4" x 12-1/2" rectangles to the sides of the block to finish piecing the center block. Press seams toward the rectangles.

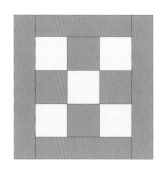

Adding the Appliqués

1. Trace 12 leaf shapes onto the paper side of the fusible web. Cut out the petals, leaving a scant 1/4" around the outside of each one. Following the manufacturer's instructions, fuse the petals to the wrong side of the second yellow fabric. Cut out each shape on the drawn line.

2. Peel the paper from the fusible web and position three petals at each corner on the right side of the center square as shown.
   Fuse the shapes in place, following the manufacturer's instructions. Finish by stitching around each petal shape with a buttonhole or zigzag stitch.

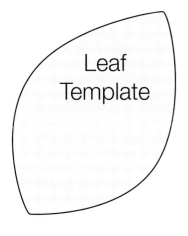

Leaf Template

walk in the woods center block

The limited use of light and dark fabrics creates a center block with visual drama.

materials

- Fat eighth or 1/6 yard of gold fabric
- Fat eighth or 1/6 yard of orange fabric

Cutting Instructions

From gold fabric, cut:
2—4-7/8" squares. Cut the squares in half diagonally to make 4 triangles.

10—2-7/8" squares. Cut the squares in half diagonally to make 20 triangles.

From orange fabric, cut:
2—4-7/8" squares. Cut the squares in half diagonally to make 4 triangles.

10—2-7/8" squares. Cut the squares in half diagonally to make 20 triangles.

Piecing the Center Block

1. Join a gold small triangle and an orange small triangle to make a triangle-square as shown. Press seam toward the orange triangle. Repeat to make 12 triangle-squares.

Make 12

2. Arrange 3 triangle-squares from Step 1, 2 gold small triangles, and 2 orange small triangles as shown. Sew the triangles to the triangle-squares in rows. Press seams toward the triangle-squares. Sew the rows together; press seams in one direction.

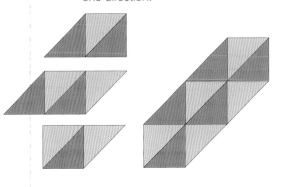

3. Join a gold large triangle and an orange large triangle to complete the block as shown. Press seams toward the large triangles. Repeat Steps 2 and 3 to make a total of 4 blocks.

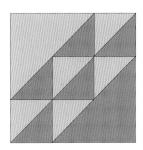

Make 4

4. Lay out the blocks, taking care to position them in the direction shown. Sew the blocks together in pairs; press seams in opposite directions. Sew the pairs together to complete the center block. Press.

sawtooth star center block

Star blocks are a favorite among quilters. Sew a sawtooth star center block and experiment with surrounding it with pieced star border blocks.

materials

- 1/8 yard of light fabric
- 1/4 yard of dark fabric

Cutting Instructions

From light fabric, cut:
1 – 3-1/2" x 42" strip.
  From the strip, cut:
  4 – 3-1/2" x 6-1/2" rectangles.
  4 – 3-1/2" squares.

From dark fabric, cut:
1 – 6-1/2" square.

8—3-1/2" squares.

Piecing the Center Block

1. Draw a diagonal line on the wrong side of 8 dark 3-1/2" squares.

2. With right sides together, align a dark 3-1/2" square with the right end of a light 3-1/2" x 6-1/2" rectangle as shown. Sew on the drawn line and trim the seam allowance to 1/4". Press seams toward the small triangle.

3. Sew another dark 3-1/2" square to the opposite end of the rectangle in the same manner to make a flying geese unit as shown. Repeat to make 4 matching flying geese units.

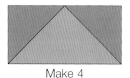

Make 4

4. Arrange the dark 6-1/2" square, 4 light 3-1/2" squares, and 4 flying geese units from Step 3 as shown. Sew the pieces together in rows. Press seams toward the squares.

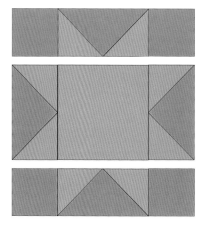

5. Sew the rows together to complete the center block. Press seams in one direction.

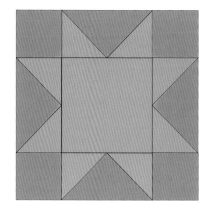

double star center block

Double the star power in a border sampler with this center block stitched up in stunning batiks.

materials

- Fat eighth or 1/6 yard of batik fabric for center star
- 1/4 yard of batik fabric for outer star
- 1/6 yard of batik fabric for background

Cutting Instructions

From center star fabric, cut:

1—4-1/2" square.

8—2-1/2" squares.

From outer star fabric, cut:

2—2-1/2" x 42" strips.
   From the strips, cut:
   4—2-1/2" x 4-1/2" rectangles.
   12—2-1/2" squares.
4—2-7/8"squares. Cut the squares in half diagonally to make 8 triangles.

From background fabric, cut:

1—2-1/2" x 42" strip.
   From the strip, cut:
   4—2-1/2" x 4-1/2" rectangles.
   4—2-1/2" squares.
4—2-7/8" squares. Cut the squares in half diagonally to make 8 triangles.

Piecing the Center Block

1. Join an outer star triangle and a background triangle to make a triangle-square as shown. Press seams away from the background triangle. Repeat to make 12 triangle-squares.

Make 12

2. Arrange 2 triangle-squares from Step 1, an outer star 2-1/2" square, and a background 2-1/2" square as shown. Sew together the squares and triangle-squares in rows. Press seams toward the squares. Sew the rows together to complete one corner unit; press seams one direction. Repeat to make 4 corner units.

Make 4

3. Draw a diagonal line on the wrong side of 8 center star 2-1/2" squares.

4. With right sides together, align a center star 2-1/2" square with the right end of an outer star 2-1/2" x 4-1/2" rectangle as shown. Sew on the drawn line and trim the seam allowance to 1/4". Press seams toward the small triangle.

5. Sew another center star 2-1/2" square to the opposite end of the rectangle in the same manner to make a flying geese unit as shown. Repeat to make 4 matching flying geese units.

Make 4

6. Repeat Steps 3-5 with 8 outer star 2-1/2" squares and 4 background 2-1/2" x 4-1/2" rectangles to make 4 additional flying geese units as shown.

Make 4

7. Sew the flying geese units from Step 5 and 6 together to make 4 flying geese pairs as shown.

Make 4

8. Arrange the center star 4-1/2" square, 4 corner units from Step 2, and 4 flying geese pairs from Step 7 as shown. Sew the pieces together in rows. Press seams toward the corner units and the center star square. Sew the rows together to complete the center block. Press seams in one direction.

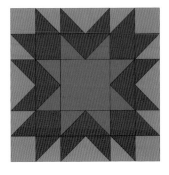

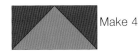

dutchman's puzzle center block

Flying geese units sewn in pairs and placed in alternating patterns create a Dutchman's Puzzle center block. Choose multiple fabrics to achieve a more colorful center block.

materials

- 1/4 yard of light fabric
- 1/4 yard of dark fabric

Cutting Instructions

From light fabric, cut:
2—3-1/2" x 42" strips.
  From the strips, cut:
  16—3-1/2" squares.

From dark fabric, cut:
2—3-1/2" x 42" strips.
  From the strips, cut:
  8—3-1/2" x 6-1/2" rectangles.

Piecing the Center Block

1. Draw a diagonal line on the wrong side of 16 light 3-1/2" squares.

2. With right sides together, align a light 3-1/2" square with the right end of a dark 3-1/2" x 6-1/2" rectangle as shown. Sew on the drawn line and trim the seam allowance to 1/4". Press seams toward the small triangle.

3. Sew another light 3-1/2" square to the opposite end of the rectangle in the same manner to make a flying geese unit as shown. Repeat to make 8 matching flying geese units.

Make 8

4. Sew the flying geese units from Step 3 together to make 4 flying geese pairs as shown.

Make 4

5. Arrange the 4 flying geese pairs as shown. Sew the pairs together in rows. Press seams in opposite directions.

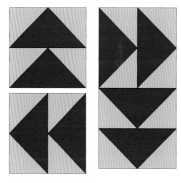

6. Sew the rows together to complete the center block. Press seams in one direction.

getting started—pieced borders

Creating a pieced border is simple and can have a huge visual impact on the overall look of a quilt. The pieced border directions in this section are designed to build a border sampler around a 12" center block. Adding borders in a 2", 4", 6", 4", and 6" sequence will create a 56-1/2" square quilt center before binding. Refer to Building a Border Sampler on pages 54 - 55 and to the Border Sampler quilt diagrams on pages 57, 59, and 61 before beginning. You will note that each of the sampler quilts includes 2—4" borders and 2—6" borders. You may interchange or substitute border blocks, but be sure to follow the border size sequence given to create a border sampler quilt.

Once you are more familiar with the process, play with different block and border styles to create your own one-of-a-kind look. Below are samples of borders you will learn in this section.

2" Squares-in-a-Row border is a wonderful way to use up scraps. I precut squares from my leftovers and store in boxes that are labeled. When a scrappy border is needed fabrics that complement my quilt center can be pulled and used in the border.

4" Broken Dishes border is made up of triangle squares. There are many triangle options that add direction to your border. Keep the viewer's eye moving and they will look at the quilt longer.

6" Maple Leaves border is another border that keeps the eye moving around the quilt center. It is one of six options given for the 6" finished quilt borders.

4" Diamonds-in-a-Row border may look difficult, but it is simple when you break the blocks into manageable units. Diamond blocks can also be joined in an alternating pattern to create a zigzag look.

6" Appliqué borders will soften the edge of a quilt center. Mix appliqué with a pieced border or cornerstones to change a quilt's look.

mitered border

A mitered border works well with stripe, plaid, or large scale fabrics. Mitered borders are the perfect background for an appliqué border.

Refer to
Building a Border Sampler on
pages 54 - 55 before beginning.

materials

• 1/6 yard of fabric

Cutting Instructions

From fabric, cut:
2—2-1/2" x 42" strips.
   From the strips, cut:
   4—2-1/2" x 20" strips.

Adding the Border

Sew the 2-1/2" x 20" strips to the center block following the Mitered Border instructions on pages 20 - 21. Quilt center, including center block and 2" border, should now measure 16-1/2" square.

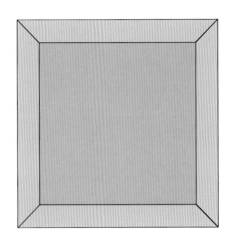

even wrap border

An even wrap border has sides that are all wrapped the same direction. A partial seam is required on the first side that is attached. Use this border with directional fabrics.

Refer to
Building a Border Sampler on
pages 54 - 55 before beginning.

materials

• 1/6 yard of fabric

Cutting Instructions

From fabric, cut:
2—2-1/2" x 42" strips.
   From the strips, cut:
   4—2-1/2" x 14" strips.

Adding the Border

Sew the 2-1/2" x 14" strips to the center block following the Even Wrap Border instructions on page 19. Quilt center, including center block and 2" border, should now measure 16-1/2" square.

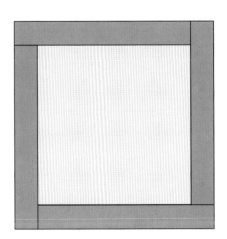

squares-in-a-row border

The squares-in-a-row border is a great way to use fabrics from your stash. Choose a variety of colors to complement the quilt center.

Border #1 Option
Finished Border Width—2"

Refer to
Building a Border Sampler on
pages 54 - 55 before beginning.

materials

- Scraps of 7 fabrics

Cutting Instructions

From scraps of fabric, cut:
4—2-1/2" squares from each fabric.

Piecing the Border

1. Join 6 – 2-1/2" squares to make top border strip. Press seams in one direction. Repeat for bottom border.

Make 2

2. Sew together the remaining 2-1/2" squares in sets of 8 to make two side border strips. Press seams in one direction.

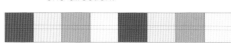

Make 2

Adding the Border

1. Add the pieced top and bottom border strips to the quilt center as shown. Press seams away from the center.

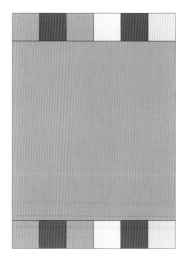

2. Add the pieced side border strips to the quilt center. Press seams away from center. Quilt center, including center block and 2" border, should now measure 16-1/2" square.

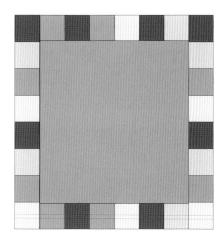

top-and-bottom wrap border

The top-and-bottom wrap borders can be made by sewing the top and bottom border strips first or the side border strips. This border works for all fabrics.

Border #1 Option Finished Border Width—2"

Refer to Building a Border Sampler on pages 54 - 55 before beginning.

materials
- 1/6 yard of fabric

Cutting Instructions

From fabric, cut:
2—2-1/2" x 42" strips.
  From the strip, cut:
  2—2-1/2" x 12-1/2" strips.
  2—2-1/2" x 14-1/2" strips.

Adding the Border

Sew the 2-1/2" x 12-1/2" strips and the 2-1/2" x 14-1/2" strips to the quilt center following the Top-and-Bottom Wrap Border instructions on page 18. Quilt center, including center block and 2" border, should now measure 16-1/2" square.

log cabin wrap border

The log cabin wrap border is a great way to use fabrics from the quilt center. Each side can be a different fabric and when used with a log cabin quilt, it continues the piecing style into the border.

Border #1 Option Finished Border Width—2"

Refer to Building a Border Sampler on pages 54 - 55 before beginning.

materials
- 2-1/2"-wide strips of four fabrics

Cutting Instructions

From fabric strips, cut:
1—2-1/2" x 12-1/2" A strip.
1—2-1/2" x 14-1/2" B strip.
1—2-1/2" x 14-1/2" C strip.
1—2-1/2" x 16-1/2" D strip.

Adding the Border

Sew the A, B, C, and D strips to the quilt center following the Log Cabin Wrap Border instructions on page 19. Quilt center, including center block and 2" border, should now measure 16-1/2" square.

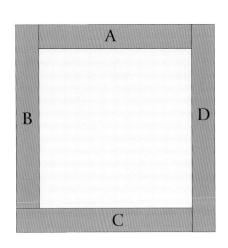

cornerstone border

Cornerstones in the border can be as simple as taking a color from the quilt center or repeating an entire block. An appliqué design is another way to give visual appeal to the border.

**Border #1 Option
Finished Border Width—2"**

*Refer to
Building a Border Sampler on
pages 54 - 55 before beginning.*

materials

- 1/6 yard of fabric
- Fabric scraps for cornerstones

Cutting Instructions

From fabric, cut:
2—2-12" x 42" strips.
  From the strips, cut:
  4—2-1/2" x 12-1/2" strips.

From fabric scrap, cut:
4—2-1/2" squares.

Adding the Border

1. Sew a 2-1/2" x 12-1/2" strip to the top and bottom edges of the quilt center. Press seams away from the center.

2. Add 1—2-1/2" square to each end of the two remaining 2-1/2" x 12-1/2" strips. Press the seams toward the strips.

Make 2

3. Sew borders to the side edges of the quilt center. Press seams away from center. Quilt center, including center block and 2" border, should now measure 16-1/2" square.

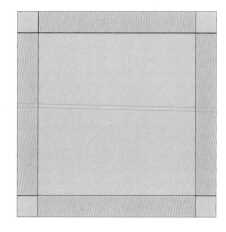

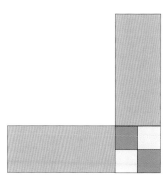

Pieced Cornerstone

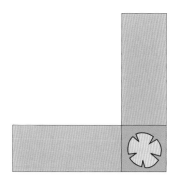

Appliquéd Cornerstone

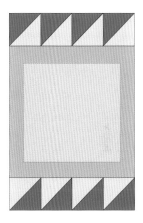

sawtooth border with cornerstones

Sawtooth borders are made up of triangle squares. Use a range of fabrics taken from the quilt's center for a more scrappy look.

*Refer to
Building a Border Sampler on
pages 54 - 55 before beginning.*

materials

- 1/4 yard or scraps of light fabric
- 1/4 yard of dark fabric
- 4—4-1/2" squares of dark fabric for cornerstones

Cutting Instructions

From light fabric, cut:
8—4-7/8" squares.
Cut squares in half diagonally to make 16 triangles.

From dark fabric, cut:
8—4-7/8" squares.
Cut the squares in half diagonally to make 16 triangles.

Piecing the Border

1. Join 1 light triangle and 1 dark triangle to make a triangle-square. Press seam toward the dark triangle. Repeat to make 16 triangle-squares.

2. Sew the triangle-squares together in sets of 4 as shown to make 4 pieced border strips. Press seams in one direction.

Adding the Border

1. Sew a border strip to the top and bottom edges of the quilt center. Press seams away from center.

2. Add 1—4-1/2" square cornerstone to each end of the two remaining pieced border strips. Press the seams away from the cornerstones. Add borders to the side edges of the quilt center. Press seams away from center. The quilt center, including center block, 2" and 4" borders, should now measure 24-1/2" square.

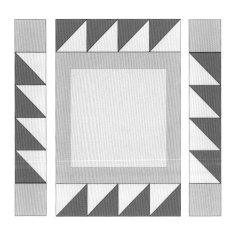

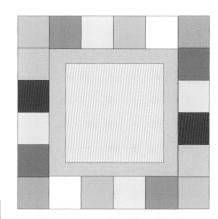

scrappy squares-in-a-row border

A quick and easy way to frame a quilt center is the squares-in-a-row border. Squares can be arranged in a random or repeating order.

Border #2 Option
Finished Border Width—4"

Refer to
Building a Border Sampler on
pages 54 - 55 before beginning.

materials

• Variety of fabric scraps

Cutting Instructions

From fabric scraps, cut:
20—4-1/2" squares.

Piecing the Border

1. Join 4—4-1/2" squares to make top border strip. Press seams in one direction. Repeat for bottom border strip.

Make 2

2. Join 6—4-1/2" squares to make 1 side border strip. Press seams in one direction. Make 2 side border strips.

Make 2

Adding the Border

1. Add the pieced top and bottom border strips to the quilt center as shown. Press seams away from center.

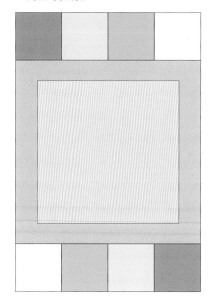

2. Add the pieced side border strips to the quilt center. Press seams away from center. The quilt center, including center block, 2" and 4" borders, should now measure 24-1/2" square.

four-patch border

A four-patch border is quick and easy to piece. Repeat two fabrics from the quilt center or choose a variety of fabrics to create a more scrappy look in your quilt border.

**Border #2 Option
Finished Border Width—4"**

*Refer to
Building a Border Sampler on
pages 54 - 55 before beginning.*

materials

- 1/4 yard of light fabric
- 1/4 yard of dark fabric

Cutting Instructions

From light fabric, cut:
3—2-1/2" x 42 strips.

From dark fabric, cut:
3—2-1/2" x 42 strips.

Piecing the Border

1. Sew the long edges of 1 light and 1 dark 2-1/2" x 42" strip together to make 1 strip set as shown. Repeat to make 3 strip sets. Press seams toward the dark fabric.

Make 3

2. Cut a total of 40—2-1/2"-wide segments from the strip set.

 Make 40

3. Sew the segments together in pairs, alternating lights and darks, to make 20—four-patch blocks.

 Make 20

4. Join 4 – four-patch blocks to make top border strip. Press the seams in one direction. Repeat for bottom border strip.

Make 2

5. Sew together the remaining four-patch blocks in sets of 6 to make 2 side border strips. Press seams in one direction.

Make 2

Adding the Border

1. Add the pieced top and bottom border strips to the quilt center as shown. Press seams away from center.

2. Add the pieced side border strips to the quilt center. Press seams away from center. The quilt center, including center block, 2" and 4" borders, should now measure 24-1/2" square.

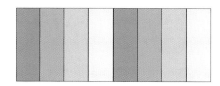

rectangles-in-a-row border with cornerstones

Rectangles are a simple way to increase the size of a quilt center. Pull fabrics from the center of your quilt for the border to create a casual look.

**Border #2 Option
Finished Border Width—4"**

*Refer to
Building a Border Sampler on
pages 54 - 55 before beginning.*

materials

- Variety of fabric scraps
- Fat eighth or 1/8 yard of fabric for cornerstones

Cutting Instructions

From fabric scraps, cut:
32—2-1/2" x 4-1/2" rectangles.

From cornerstone fabric, cut:
4—4-1/2" squares.

Piecing the Border

Sew the rectangles together in sets of 8 as shown to make 4 pieced border strips. Press seams in one direction.

Adding the Border

1. Sew a border strip to the top and bottom edges of the quilt center. Press seams away from center.

2. Add 1—4-1/2" square cornerstone to each end of the two remaining pieced border strips. Press the seams away from the cornerstones. Add borders to the side edges of the quilt center. Press seams away from center. The quilt center, including center block, 2" and 4" borders, should now measure 24-1/2" square.

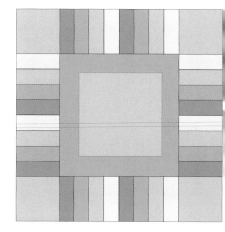

broken dishes border

Half-square triangles form the broken dishes block. Pull colors from the center of the quilt for a variety of two color blocks that add visual interest to the border.

**Border #2 Option
Finished Border Width—4"**

*Refer to
Building a Border Sampler on
pages 54 - 55 before beginning.*

materials

- 1/3 yard of light fabric
- 1/8 yard each of 4 dark fabrics

Cutting Instructions

From light fabric, cut:
3—2-7/8" x 42" strips.
From the strips, cut: 40 – 2-7/8" squares. Cut the squares in half diagonally to make 80 triangles.

From each dark fabric, cut:
1—2-7/8" x 42" strip.
From each strip, cut: 10 – 2-7/8" squares. Cut the squares in half diagonally to make 20 triangles.

Piecing the Border

1. Join 1 light and 1 dark triangle to make a triangle-square. Press seam toward the dark triangle. Repeat to make 80 triangle-squares.

Make 80

2. Arrange 4 matching triangle-squares as shown. Sew together the triangle-squares in rows. Press seams in opposite directions. Sew the rows together to complete one Broken Dishes block. Repeat to make 20 Broken Dishes blocks.

Make 20

3. Join 4 Broken Dishes blocks to make top border strip as shown. Press seams in one direction. Repeat for bottom border strip.

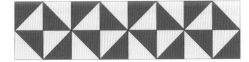

Make 2

4. Sew together the remaining Broken Dishes blocks in sets of 6 to make 2 side border strips. Press seams in one direction.

Make 2

Adding the Border

1. Add the pieced top and bottom border strips to the quilt center as shown. Press seams away from center.

2. Add the pieced side border strips to the quilt center. Press seams away from center. The quilt center, including center block, 2" and 4" borders, should now measure 24-1/2" square.

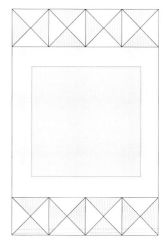

hourglass border

The hourglass block pieced in contrasting colors adds drama to the quilt center border.

**Border #2 Option
Finished Border Width—4"**

*Refer to
Building a Border Sampler on
pages 54 - 55 before beginning.*

materials

- 1/3 yard of light fabric
- 1/3 yard of dark fabric

Cutting Instructions

From light fabric, cut:
2—5-1/4" x 42" strips.
  From the strips, cut 10—5-1/4"
  squares. Cut the squares into
  quarters diagonally to make
  40 triangles.

From dark fabric, cut:
2—5-1/4" x 42" strips.
  From the strips, cut 10—5-1/4"
  squares. Cut the squares into
  quarters diagonally to make
  40 triangles.

Piecing the Border

1. Arrange 2 light and 2 dark triangles as shown. Sew together the triangles in pairs. Press seams in opposite directions. Sew the pairs together to complete one Hourglass block. Repeat to make 20 Hourglass blocks.

Make 20

2. Join 4 Hourglass blocks to make top border strip as shown. Press seams in one direction. Repeat for bottom border strip.

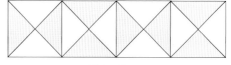

Make 2

3. Sew together the remaining Hourglass blocks in sets of 6 to make 2 side border strips. Press seams in one direction.

Make 2

Adding the Border

1. Add the pieced top and bottom border strips to the quilt center as shown. Press seams away from center.

2. Add the pieced side border strips to the quilt center. Press seams away from center. The quilt center, including center block, 2" and 4" borders, should now measure 24-1/2" square.

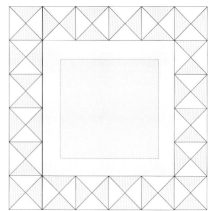

maple leaves border

Maple leaves surrounding a quilt center are a great addition to a fall-themed quilt.

*Refer to
Building a Border Sampler on
pages 54 - 55 before beginning.*

materials

- 1/2 yard of light fabric for background
- 1/4 yard each of 5 dark fabrics for leaves

Cutting Instructions

From light fabric, cut:

3—2-7/8" x 42" strips.
From the strips, cut:
40—2-7/8" squares. Cut the squares in half diagonally to make 80 large triangles.

2—2-5/8" x 42" strips.
From the strips, cut:
20—2-5/8" squares. Cut the squares in half diagonally to make 40 small triangles.

2—2-1/2" x 42" strips.
From the strips, cut:
20—2-1/2" squares.

From each dark fabric, cut:

1—2-7/8" x 42" strip.
From the strip, cut:
8—2-7/8" squares. Cut the squares in half diagonally to make 16 large triangles.

1—2-1/2" x 42" strip.
From the strip, cut:
4—2-1/2" x 4-1/2" rectangles.
4—2-1/2" squares.

1—1" x 42" strip.
From the strip, cut:
4—1" x 4" rectangles.

Piecing the Border

1. Center and sew a light small triangle on a dark 1" x 4" strip. Repeat with a second small triangle on the opposite edge of the dark strip to complete a stem square. Press the seams toward the strip. Trim the ends of the strip so the stem square measures 2-1/2" square. Repeat to make 20 stem squares.

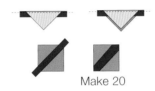

Make 20

2. Join 1 light large triangle and 1 dark large triangle to make a triangle-square. Press seam toward the dark triangle. Repeat to make 80 triangle-squares.

Make 80

3. Using matching fabrics, arrange 4 triangle-squares, 1—dark 2-1/2" x 4-1/2" rectangle, 1 light 2-1/2" square, 1 dark 2-1/2" square, and 1 stem square as shown. Sew together the pieces in rows. Press seams in the same direction within each row, alternating directions from row to row. Sew the rows together to complete one Maple Leaf block. Block should measure 6-1/2" square. Repeat to make 4 blocks with each dark fabric for a total of 20 Maple Leaf blocks.

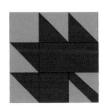

Make 20

4. Join 4 Maple Leaf blocks to make top border strip, varying the direction of the leaves. Press seams in one direction. Repeat for bottom border.

Make 2

5. Sew together the remaining Maple Leaf blocks in sets of 6 to make 2 side border strips. Press seams in one direction.

Make 2

Adding the Border

1. Add the pieced top and bottom border strips to the quilt center as shown. Press seams away from center.

2. Add the pieced side border strips to the quilt center. Press seams away from center. The quilt center, including center block, 2", 4" and 6" borders, should now measure 36-1/2" square.

pinwheel border

A pinwheel border gives a quilt the illusion of movement. Choose two similar colors from the center block or a variety of complementary colors to make the pieced pinwheel blocks.

*Refer to
Building a Border Sampler on
pages 54 - 55 before beginning.*

materials

- 1/2 yard of light fabric
- 1/8 yard each of 4 dark fabrics

Cutting Instructions

From light fabric, cut:
4—3-7/8" x 42" strips.
    From the strips, cut: 40—3-7/8" squares; cut the squares in half diagonally to make 80 triangles.

From each dark fabric, cut:
1—3-7/8" x 42" strip.
    From each strip, cut: 10—3-7/8" squares; cut the squares in half diagonally to make 20 triangles.

Piecing the Border

1. Join 1 light triangle and 1 dark triangle to make a triangle-square. Press seam toward the dark triangle. Repeat to make 80 triangle-squares.

Make 80

2. Arrange 4 matching triangle-squares as shown. Sew together the triangle-squares in rows. Press seams in opposite directions. Sew the rows together to complete one Pinwheel block. Block should measure 6-1/2" square. Repeat to make 20 Pinwheel blocks.

Make 20

3. Join 4 Pinwheel blocks to make top border strip as shown. Press seams in one direction. Repeat for bottom border.

Make 2

4. Sew together the remaining Pinwheel blocks in sets of 6 to make 2 side border strips. Press seams in one direction.

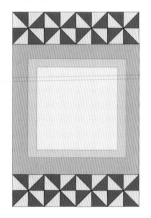

Make 2

Adding the Border

1. Add the pieced top and bottom border strips to the quilt center as shown. Press seams away from center.

2. Add the pieced side border strips to the quilt center. Press seams away from center. The quilt center, including center block, 2", 4" and 6" borders, should now measure 36-1/2" square.

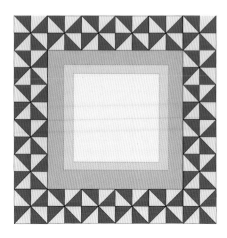

positive negative border

Positive negative blocks are pieced with light and dark fabrics. These blocks are a good way to use up leftover fabric from your center block.

**Border #3 Option
Finished Border Width—6"**

*Refer to
Building a Border Sampler on
pages 54 - 55 before beginning.*

materials

- Fat eighth or 1/8 yard each of 20 fabrics

Cutting Instructions

From each fabric, cut:
6—2-7/8" squares.
   Cut the squares in half diagonally to make 12 triangles.
3—2-1/2" squares.

Piecing the Border

1. Sort the fabric pieces into 10 pairs, selecting 2 fabrics for each pair that coordinate well together. Join the triangles from the paired fabrics to make a total of 120 triangle-squares. Press seams toward the darker triangles.

 Make 120

2. Arrange 12 matching triangle-squares and 3 – 2-1/2" squares from each of the paired fabrics as shown, creating 1 positive block and 1 negative block. Sew together the triangle-squares and squares in rows. Press seams in the same direction within each row, alternating directions from row to row. Sew the rows together to complete the blocks. Blocks should measure 6-1/2" square. Repeat to make 20 blocks.

Make 20

3. Join 4 blocks to make top border strip as shown. Press seams in one direction. Repeat for bottom border.

Make 2

4. Sew together the remaining blocks in sets of 6 to make 2 side border strips. Press seams in one direction.

Make 2

Adding the Border

1. Add the pieced top and bottom border strips to the quilt center as shown. Press seams away from center.

2. Add the pieced side border strips to the quilt center. Press seams away from center. The quilt center, including center block, 2", 4" and 6" borders, should now measure 36-1/2" square.

sawtooth star border

Sawtooth star blocks provide a great opportunity to implement all the quilt center's colors into the quilt border.

Refer to
Building a Border Sampler on
pages 54 - 55 before beginning.

materials

- Light fabric scraps totaling 3/4 yard for background
- Medium fabric scraps totaling 1/4 yard for centers
- Dark fabric scraps totaling 1/2 yard for points

Cutting Instructions

From light fabric scraps, cut:
80 – 2" squares, cutting 4 matching for each block.

80 – 2" x 3-1/2" rectangles, cutting 4 to match the light squares for each block.

From medium fabric scraps, cut:
20 – 3-1/2" squares

From dark fabric scraps, cut:
160 – 2" squares, cutting 8 matching for each block.

Piecing the Border

1. Draw a diagonal line on the wrong side of the dark 2" squares.

2. With right sides together, align a dark 2" square with the right end of a light 2" x 3-1/2" rectangle as shown. Sew on the drawn line and trim the seam to 1/4". Press seams toward the small triangle.

3. Sew a matching dark 2" square to the opposite end of the rectangle in the same manner to make a Flying Geese Unit as shown. Repeat to make 4 matching Flying Geese Units for each block for a total of 80 Flying Geese Units.

   Make 80

4. Arrange 1 medium 3-1/2" square, 4 Flying Geese units, and 4 matching 2" squares as shown. Sew the pieces together in rows. Press seams toward the squares. Sew the rows together to complete the block. Block should measure 6-1/2" square. Repeat to make 20 blocks.

   Make 20

5. Join 4 blocks to make top border strip as shown. Press seams in one direction. Repeat for bottom border.

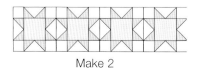

Make 2

6. Sew together the remaining blocks in sets of 6 to make 2 side border strips. Press seams in one direction.

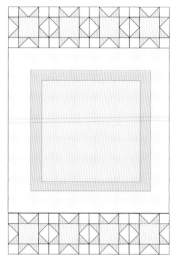

Make 2

Adding the Border

1. Add the pieced top and bottom border strips to the quilt center. Press seams away from center.

2. Add the pieced side border strips to the quilt center. Press seams away from center. The quilt center, including center block, 2", 4" and 6" borders, should now measure 36-1/2" square.

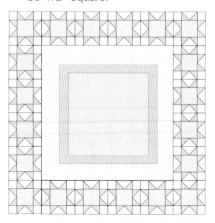

nine-patch checkerboard border

Nine-patches are quick-to-piece border blocks. Frame the center block with a variety of fabric scraps or choose a light and dark fabric.

Border #3 Option
Finished Border Width—6"

Refer to Building a Border Sampler on pages 54 - 55 before beginning.

materials

- 1/2 yard of light fabric
- 1/2 yard of dark fabric

Cutting Instructions

From light fabric, cut:
6—2-1/2" x 42" strips.

From dark fabric, cut:
6—2-1/2" x 42" strips.

Piecing the Border

1. Sew 2-1/2" x 42" dark strips to both sides of a 2-1/2" x 42" light strip to make 1 Strip Set A. Press seams toward the dark fabric. Repeat to make a second strip set.

Make 2

2. Sew 2-1/2" x 42" light strips to both sides of a 2-1/2 x 42" dark strip to make 1 Strip Set B. Press seams toward the dark fabric. Repeat to make a second strip set.

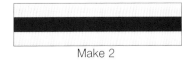

Make 2

3. Cut 30 – 2-1/2" wide segments from Strip Set A and 30 – 2-1/2" segments from Strip Set B.

  Make 30 of each

4. Arrange 2 Strip Set A segments and 1 Strip Set B segment as shown. Sew the segments together to complete 1 nine-patch A block. Press seams in one direction. Block should measure 6-1/2" square. Repeat to make 10 A blocks.

Make 10

5. Arrange 1 Strip Set A segment and 2 Strip Set B segments as shown. Sew the segments together to complete 1 B block. Press seams in one direction. Block should measure 6-1/2" square. Repeat to make 10 B blocks.

Make 10

6. Join 4 blocks to make top border strip, alternating A and B blocks as shown. Press seams in one direction. Repeat for bottom border.

Make 2

7. In the same manner, sew together the remaining blocks in sets of 6 to make 2 side border strips. Press seams in one direction.

Make 2

Adding the Border

1. Add the pieced top and bottom border strips to the quilt center. Press seams away from center.

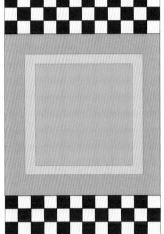

2. Add the pieced side border strips to the quilt center. Press seams away from center. The quilt center, including center block, 2", 4" and 6" borders, should now measure 36-1/2" square.

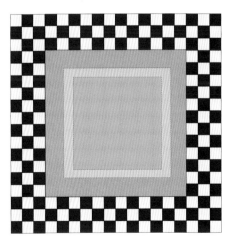

delectable mountain border

Delectable mountain blocks add drama to any quilt border. Use a two color palette or pull fabrics from your stash to enhance the center block.

Border #3 Option
Finished Border Width—6"

Refer to
Building a Border Sampler on
pages 54 - 55 before beginning.

materials

• 1 yard of dark solid fabric

• Variety of print fabric scraps for 20 blocks

Cutting Instructions

From dark fabric, cut:

2—6-7/8" strips.
   From the strips, cut:
   10—6-7/8" squares. Cut the squares in half diagonally to make 20 large triangles.

3—2-3/8" strips.
   From the strips, cut:
   40—2-3/8" squares. Cut the squares in half diagonally to make 80 small triangles.

2—2" x 42" strips.
   From the strips, cut:
   20—2" squares.

From print fabric scraps, cut:

10—3-7/8" squares.
   Cut the squares in half diagonally to make 1 medium triangle for each of the 20 blocks.

Note: *If you desire a scrappier look, cut 20 squares in half diagonally and use only 1 medium triangle of each fabric for the blocks.*

60—2-3/8" squares; cutting 3 matching for each block. Cut the squares in half diagonally to make 120 small triangles.

Piecing the Border

1. Join 1 dark small triangle and 1 print small triangle to make a triangle-square. Press seam toward the dark triangle. Repeat to make 80 triangle-squares.

Make 80

2. Using matching fabric, sew together 2 triangle-squares and 1 print triangle as shown for Unit A.

Unit A

3. Using matching fabric, sew together 2 triangle-squares, 1 print triangle, and 1 dark 2" square as shown for Unit B.

Unit B

4. Arrange Unit A, Unit B, 1 print medium triangle, and 1 dark large triangle as shown. Join Unit A to the medium triangle; press seam toward triangle. Join Unit B; press seam toward triangle. Add the dark large triangle to complete the block; press seam toward large triangle. Block should measure 6-1/2" square. Repeat Steps 2-4 to make 20 blocks.

Make 20

5. Join 4 blocks to make top border strip, positioning the blocks as shown. Press seams in one direction. Repeat for bottom border.

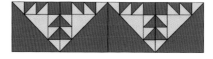
Make 2

6. In the same manner, sew together the remaining blocks in sets of 6 to make 2 side border strips. Press seams in one direction.

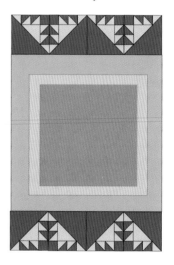
Make 2

Adding the Border

1. Add the pieced top and bottom border strips to the quilt center. Press seams away from center.

2. Add the pieced side border strips to the quilt center. Press seams away from center. The quilt center, including center block, 2", 4" and 6" borders, should now measure 36-1/2" square.

diamonds-in-a-row border with cornerstones

Diamond blocks add movement to a quilt border. They may appear difficult, but when broken down into single blocks they are actually easy.

**Border #4 Option
Finished Border Width—4"**

*Refer to
Building a Border Sampler on
pages 54 - 55 before beginning.*

materials

- 1 yard of medium fabric
- Variety of bright fabric scraps

Cutting Instructions

From medium fabric, cut:
9—2-1/2" x 42" strips.
 From the strips,
 cut 144—2-1/2" squares.
4—4-1/2" squares.

From bright fabric scraps, cut:
72—2-1/2" x 4-1/2" rectangles.

Piecing the Border

1. Draw a diagonal line on the wrong side of the medium 2-1/2" squares.

2. With right sides together, align a 2-1/2" square with one end of a bright 2-1/2" x 4-1/2" rectangle as shown. Sew on the drawn line and trim the seam to 1/4". Press seams toward the small triangle.

3. Sew a second 2-1/2" square to the opposite end of the rectangle in the same manner to make a Diamond Unit as shown. Repeat to make 72 Diamond Units.

Make 72

4. Sew the Diamond Units together in sets of 18 as shown to make 4 pieced border strips. Press seams in one direction.

Make 4

Adding the Border

1. Sew a border strip to the top and bottom edges of the quilt center. Press seams away from the center.

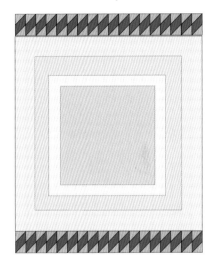

2. Add 1 – 4-1/2" square to each end of the two remaining pieced border strips for the cornerstones. Press the seams away from the cornerstones. Add borders to the side edges of the quilt center. Press seams away from the center. Quilt center, including center block, 2", 4", 6" and 4" borders, should now measure 44-1/2" square.

zigzag border with cornerstones

Diamond blocks offer numerous border possibilities when arranged in different patterns.

Refer to
Building a Border Sampler on
pages 54 - 55 before beginning.

materials

- 1 yard of medium fabric
- Variety of bright fabric scraps

Cutting Instructions

From medium fabric, cut:
9—2-1/2" x 42" strips.
    From the strips, cut 144 – 2-1/2" squares.

4—4-1/2" squares.

From bright fabric scraps, cut:
72—2-1/2" x 4-1/2" rectangles.

Piecing the Border

1. Draw a diagonal line on the wrong side of the medium 2-1/2" squares.

2. With right sides together, align a 2-1/2" square with one end of a bright 2-1/2" x 4-1/2" rectangle as shown. Sew on the drawn line and trim the seam to 1/4". Press seams toward the small triangle.

3. Sew a second 2-1/2" square to the opposite end of the rectangle in the same manner to make a Diamond A Unit as shown. Repeat to make 36 Diamond A Units.

Make 36

4. Repeat Steps 2-3 to make 36 Diamond B Units as shown.

Make 36

5. Sew the diamond units together in sets of 18 to make 4 pieced border strips, alternating the Diamond A and B Units as shown. Press seams in one direction.

Adding the Border

1. Sew a border strip to the top and bottom edges of the quilt center. Press seams away from the center.

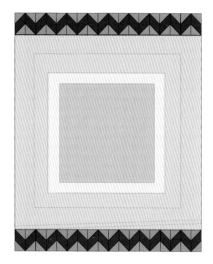

2. Add 1 – 4-1/2" square to each end of the two remaining pieced border strips for the cornerstones. Press the seams away from the cornerstones. Add borders to the side edges of the quilt center. Press seams away from the center. Quilt center, including center block, 2", 4", 6" and 4" borders, should now measure 44-1/2" square.

Make 4

basket weave border

Simple rectangles pieced together and placed in alternating directions create a basket weave border.

Refer to
Building a Border Sampler on
pages 54 - 55 before beginning.

materials

- Variety of similar value and tone fabric scraps

Cutting Instructions

From fabric scraps, cut:
80—2-1/2" x 4-1/2" rectangles.

Piecing the Border

1. Join two rectangles to make a Basket Weave Unit as shown. Press the seam in one direction. Repeat to make 40 Basket Units.

Make 40

2. Join 9 Basket Weave Units to make top border strip, alternating the direction of the units as shown. Press seams in one direction. Repeat for bottom border strip.

Make 2

3. Sew together the remaining Basket Weave Units in sets of 11 to make 2 side border strips. Press seams in one direction.

Make 2

Adding the Border

1. Add the pieced top and bottom border strips to the quilt center as shown. Press seams away from center.

5. Add the pieced side border strips to the quilt center. Press seams away from center. Quilt center, including center block, 2", 4", 6" and 4" borders, should now measure 44-1/2" square.

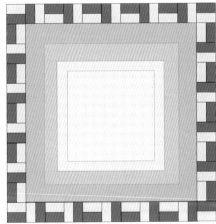

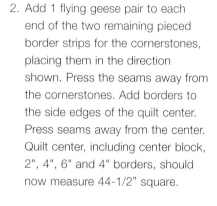

flying geese border

Flying geese blocks add a feeling of motion around the edge of a center block. You can achieve completely different looks by using a multitude of scrap fabrics or a simple two-color palette.

Refer to
Building a Border Sampler on
pages 54 - 55 before beginning.

materials

- 1 yard of medium fabric
- Bright fabric scraps

Cutting Instructions

From medium fabric, cut:
10—2-1/2" x 42" strips.
From the strips,
cut 160—2-1/2" squares.

From bright fabric scraps, cut:
80—2-1/2" x 4-1/2" rectangles.

Piecing the Border

1. Draw a diagonal line on the wrong side of the medium 2-1/2" squares.

2. With right sides together, align a medium 2-1/2" square with the right end of a 2-1/2" x 4-1/2" rectangle as shown. Sew on the drawn line and trim the seam to 1/4". Press seams toward the small triangle.

3. Sew a second 2-1/2" square to the opposite end of the rectangle in the same manner to make a flying geese unit as shown. Repeat to make 80 flying geese units.

Make 80

4. Join 18 flying geese units to make top border strip. Press the seams in one direction. Repeat for bottom border strip.

Make 2

5. Sew together the remaining flying geese units in 2 sets of 20 and 2 pairs. Press the seams in one direction. Add 1 pair to the right end of each 20-unit strip in the direction shown to complete the side border strips. Press the seams away from the pairs.

Make 2

Adding the Border

1. Sew a border strip to the top and bottom edges of the quilt center. Press seams away from the center.

2. Add 1 flying geese pair to each end of the two remaining pieced border strips for the cornerstones, placing them in the direction shown. Press the seams away from the cornerstones. Add borders to the side edges of the quilt center. Press seams away from the center. Quilt center, including center block, 2", 4", 6" and 4" borders, should now measure 44-1/2" square.

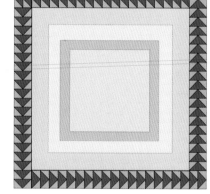

sawtooth border with cornerstones

This variation of the sawtooth block uses two different sizes of triangles. Use three fabrics in complementary colors to create a border that keeps the eye moving.

**Border #4 Option
Finished Border Width—4"**

*Refer to
Building a Border Sampler on
pages 54 - 55 before beginning.*

materials

- 1/3 yard of light fabric
- 1/3 yard of medium fabric
- 1/2 yard of dark fabric

Cutting Instructions

From light fabric, cut:
2—5-1/4" x 42" strips.
    From the strips, cut:
    9—5-1/4" squares. Cut the
    squares into quarters diagonally
    to make 36 small triangles.

From medium fabric, cut:
2—5-1/4" x 42" strips.
    From the strips, cut:
    9—5-1/4" squares. Cut the
    squares into quarters diagonally
    to make 36 small triangles.

From dark fabric, cut:
3—4-7/8" x 42" strips.
    From the strips, cut:
    18—4-7/8" squares. Cut the
    squares in half diagonally
    to make 36 large triangles.
4—4-1/2" squares.

Piecing the Border

1. Sew together the light and medium small triangles in pairs to make 18 A Pairs and 18 B Pairs as shown. Press the seams toward the medium triangles.

Make 18   Make 18

2. Add a dark large triangle to each pair, completing 18 A Units and 18 B Units.

Make 18   Make 18

3. Join 9 A Units to make top border strip. Press the seams in one direction. Repeat for bottom border strip.

Make 2

4. Sew together the B Units in 2 sets of 9; press the seams in one direction. Add 1 dark 4-1/2" square to each end of the B Unit strips to complete the side border strips. Press the seams away from the squares.

Make 2

Adding the Border

1. Sew the pieced top and bottom border strips to the quilt center in the direction shown. Press seams away from the center.

2. Add pieced side border strips to the quilt center in the direction shown. Press seams away from the center. Quilt center, including center block, 2", 4", 6" and 4" borders, should now measure 44-1/2" square.

optional border block sizes

I have provided a few alternatives to the border block sizes offered. Mix and match border blocks and sizes to give your quilt center a one-of-a-kind frame. If you are making the sampler quilt you can substitute the blocks used, but be sure to follow the border size sequence given.

Sawtooth

Color	Shape	Cut	Subcut	— finished size —		
				2"	3"	6"
Dark	A - 1 h/s triangle	1	1	2-7/8"	3-7/8"	6-7/8"
Light	A - 1 h/s triangle	1	1	2-7/8"	3-7/8"	6-7/8"

Four-Patch

Color	Shape	Cut	— finished size —		
			2"	3"	6"
Dark	A - 2 squares	2	1-1/2"	2"	3-1/2"
Light	A - 2 squares	2	1-1/2"	2"	3-1/2"

Broken Dishes

Color	Shape	Cut	Subcut	— finished size —		
				3"	4"	6"
Dark	A - 4 h/s triangles	2	4	2-3/8"	2-7/8"	3-7/8"
Light	A - 4 h/s triangles	2	4	2-3/8"	2-7/8"	3-7/8"

Hourglass

Color	Shape	Cut	Subcut	— finished size —		
				3"	4"	6"
Dark	A - 2 q/s triangles	1	2	4-1/4"	5-1/4"	7-1/4"
Light	A - 2 q/s triangles	1	2	4-1/4"	5-1/4"	7-1/4"

Pinwheel

Color	Shape	Cut	Subcut	— finished size —		
				3"	4"	6"
Dark	A - 4 h/s triangles	2	4	2-3/8"	2-7/8"	3-7/8"
Light	A - 4 h/s triangles	2	4	2-3/8"	2-7/8"	3-7/8"

Nine-Patch

Color	Shape	Cut	— finished size —	
			3"	6"
Dark	A - 5 squares	5	1-1/2"	2-1/2"
Light	A - 4 squares	4	1-1/2"	2-1/2"

Diamonds

Color	Shape	Cut	— finished size —	
			2"x4"	3"x6"
Dark	A - 1 rectangle	1	2-1/2"x4-1/2"	3-1/2"x6-1/2"
Light	B - 2 squares	2	2-1/2"	3-1/2"

Basket Weave

Color	Shape	Cut	— finished size —		
			2"	3"	4"
Dark	A - 1 rectangle	1	1-1/2"x2-1/2"	2"x3-1/2"	2-1/2"x4-1/2"
Light	A - 1 rectangle	1	1-1/2"x2-1/2"	2"x3-1/2"	2-1/2"x4-1/2"

Flying Geese

Color	Shape	Cut	— finished size —	
			2"x4"	3"x6"
Dark	A - 1 rectangle	1	2-1/2"x4-1/2"	3-1/2"x6-1/2"
Light	B - 2 squares	2	2-1/2"	3-1/2"

Three-Piece Sawtooth

Color	Shape	Cut	Subcut	— finished size —		
				3"	4"	6"
Dark	A - 1 h/s triangle	1	1	3-7/8"	4-7/8"	6-7/8"
Medium	B - 1 q/s triangle	1	1	4-1/4"	5-1/4"	7-1/4"
Light	B - 1 q/s triangle	1	1	4-1/4"	5-1/4"	7-1/4"

Note: If you decide to follow a different border sequence or have enlarged your center block, you will need to break the border down into blocks or units that are mathematically divisible into your quilt center.

getting started—appliqué borders

Appliqué shapes can be added to any style quilt border. The borders provided here are 6" finished basic borders, but don't be afraid to venture beyond and embellish pieced borders with shapes and vines appropriate for the quilt center.

Even Wrap borders, top-and-bottom wrap, and log cabin wrap borders provide a good background for appliqué pieces scattered randomly along the edges. Pull colors from the center of the quilt and repeat them in the appliqué shapes.

Mitered borders allow you to place an appliqué shape directly on the seam line without making it appear bulky. You may then hand or machine appliqué the pieces in place.

Cornerstone borders, when enhanced with a vine and flower appliqué, soften a quilt's edges and give it a feeling of movement. You may appliqué the shapes onto the borders before sewing them to your quilt center.

log cabin wrap border

Pull four favorite fabrics from the quilt center and use them in a log cabin wrap border. Scraps of fabric from the center may also be used to create the appliqué pieces.

Border #5 Option
Finished Border Width—6"

Refer to
Building a Border Sampler on
pages 54 - 55 before beginning.

materials

- 1-3/4 yards of fabric

- Assorted fabric scraps for appliqué

Cutting Instructions

From fabric, cut:

1—6-1/2" x 44-1/2" A strip from lengthwise grain.

1—6-1/2" x 50-1/2" B strip from lengthwise grain.

1—6-1/2" x 50-1/2" C strip from lengthwise grain.

1—6-1/2" x 56-1/2" D strip from lengthwise grain.

Adding the Border

1. Sew the A border strip to the top edge of the quilt center. Press toward the border.

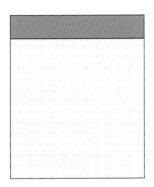

2. Sew the B border strip to the left side of the quilt center. Press toward the border.

3. Sew the C border strip to the bottom edge of the quilt center. Press toward the border.

4. Sew the D border strip to the right side of the quilt center. Press toward the border.

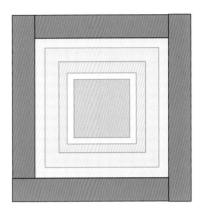

5. Quilt center, including center block, 2", 4", 6", 4" and 6" borders, should now measure 56-1/2" square.

6. Use the desired appliqué patterns on pages 100 - 106 and the method of your choice to appliqué shapes onto the border.

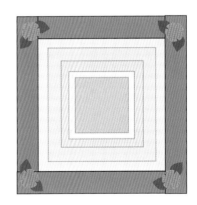

top-and-bottom wrap border

The top-and-bottom wrap border is the most basic. It requires less yardage than other border styles, but provides a nice canvas for appliqué shapes.

Border #5 Option
Finished Border Width—6"

Refer to
Building a Border Sampler on
pages 54 - 55 before beginning.

materials

- 1-3/4 yards of fabric
- Assorted fabric scraps for appliqué

Cutting Instructions

From fabric, cut:
2—6-1/2" x 44-1/2" strips from lengthwise grain.

2—6-1/2" x 56-1/2" strips from lengthwise grain.

Adding the Border

1. Sew the 6-1/2" x 44-1/2" border strips to the top and bottom of the quilt center using 1/4" seam allowance. Press toward the border strips.

2. Sew the 6-1/2" x 56-1/2" side border strips to the sides of the quilt center using 1/4" seam allowance. Press toward the border strips.

3. Quilt center, including center block, 2", 4", 6", 4" and 6" borders, should now measure 56-1/2" square.

4. Use the desired appliqué patterns on pages 100 - 106 and the method of your choice to appliqué shapes onto the border.

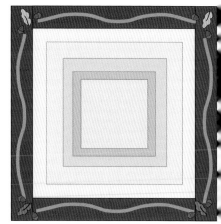

even wrap border

Wrapping all the borders in the same direction allows the viewer's eye to keep moving around the quilt center. Add an appliqué vine or scatter random shapes along the border.

**Border #5 Option
Finished Border Width—6"**

*Refer to
Building a Border Sampler on
pages 54 - 55 before beginning.*

materials

- 1-1/2 yards of fabric
- Assorted fabric scraps for appliqué

Cutting Instructions

From fabric, cut:
4—6-1/2" x 50-1/2" strips cut from lengthwise grain.

Adding the Border

1. Sew one border strip to the top of the quilt center using a partial seam and 1/4" seam allowance. Press toward the border strip.

2. Continue adding the border strips to the quilt center, as shown. Press seams toward the border strips.

3. Sew the final border strip to the quilt center and press. Finish sewing the partial seam to connect the borders.

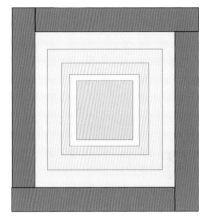

4. Quilt center, including center block, 2", 4", 6", 4" and 6" borders, should now measure 56-1/2" square.

5. Use the desired appliqué patterns on pages 100 - 106 and the method of your choice to appliqué shapes onto the border.

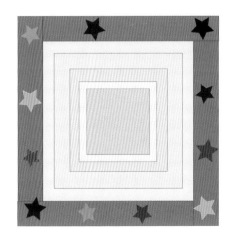

mitered border

Borders with mitered corners provide a good backdrop for appliqué pieces. Mitered borders flow around a quilt and allow the appliqué to stand out.

Border #5 Option
Finished Border Width—6"

Refer to
Building a Border Sampler on
pages 54 - 55 before beginning.

materials

- 1-3/4 yards of fabric
- Assorted fabric scraps for appliqué

Cutting Instructions

From fabric, cut:
4—6-1/2" x 62" border strips cut from lengthwise grain

Adding the Border

1. Mark 1/4" from each end of the border strips using pins or a marking tool.

2. Fold the border strips in half lengthwise to find the centers. Mark with a pin or marking tool.

3. Measure half the finished size measurement on each side of the center marked point. Fold in half between center and outer marked point. Mark with a pin or marking tool.

4. Mark 1/4" on each corner of the quilt top using a pin or marking tool.

5. Fold the quilt top in half and mark the center of each side with a pin or marking tool.

6. Fold the quilt top in half again from the marked center point to the edge of the quilt top. Mark the center point with a pin or marking tool.

Note: *You should now have five marked points to match and align the border on your quilt center.*

7. Pin the borders to the quilt center matching the marked points.

8. Beginning and ending at the corner with the marked 1/4" point, backstitch and sew the border strip to the quilt center.

9. Repeat for the remaining borders.

10. Press the seam towards the border.

Mitering the Corners

1. Working on the ironing board, lay one border vertically on the board.

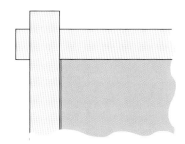

2. Bring the adjoining border up and fold at a 45-degree angle. It should lay on top of the border in Step 1. Press.

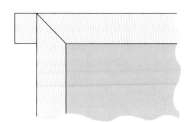

3. Fold the quilt center on the diagonal, right sides together.

4. The pressed border should now be laying flat on top of the other border strip. Pin along creased line.

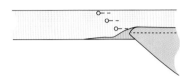

5. Stitch on the creased line, backstitching 1/4" from the edges. Trim seam to 1/4". Press.

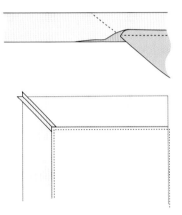

6. Repeat for remaining corners.

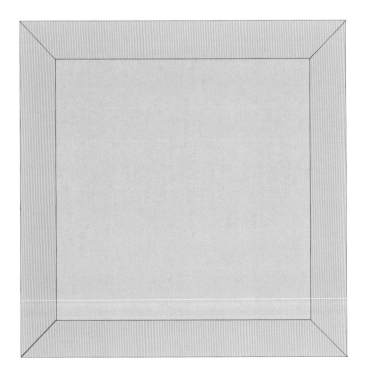

7. Quilt center, including center block, 2", 4", 6", 4" and 6" borders, should now measure 56-1/2" square.

8. .Use the desired appliqué patterns on pages 100 - 106 and the method of your choice to appliqué shapes onto the border.

cornerstone border with vine

Adding cornerstones to a border creates many ways to dramatize your quilt center. Repeat a pieced block from the quilt center in the corner, appliqué the cornerstones with a simple design, or pull in a favorite complementary color.

Border #5 Option
Finished Border Width—6"

Refer to
Building a Border Sampler on
pages 54 - 55 before beginning.

materials

- 1 1/4 yards of fabric for border

- Fat quarter or 1/4 yard of fabric for cornerstones

- 6 yards of 1-1/2"-wide bias strips for vines (optional)

- Assorted fabric scraps for appliqué

Cutting Instructions

From border fabric, cut:
4—6-1/2" x 44-1/2" strips
   cut from lengthwise grain.

From cornerstone fabric, cut:
4—6-1/2" squares.

Adding the Border

1. If vine is desired, sew together the optional bias strips to make one long strip; press the seams open. Handle bias strip gently to retain the stretch for placement on border. With wrong sides together, finger press 1/3 of the width up. Fold remaining fabric over the first edge, folding the strip in thirds. Press. Cut the strip into 4 equal lengths for the vines.

Note: *If you prefer a finished vine in a different width, see page 42 for directions.*

2. Fold a light 6-1/2" x 44-1/2" border strip in half, aligning the short edges. Fold strip in half again in the same direction. Press along the fold lines, dividing the strip into quarters. Use pins to mark the border strip 1-1/2" below the top edge at the side edges and at the center fold. Also, mark 1-1/2" above the bottom edge at the two remaining fold lines as shown.

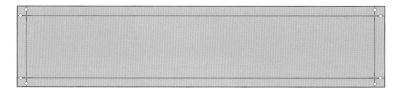

3. Position a vine strip on the marked border strip, beginning at the top left pin, gently curving it from pin to pin, and ending at the top right pin. Baste or firmly pin the vine in place. Hand- or machine-stitch the vine in place. Repeat Steps 2 and 3 with the 3 remaining border strips.

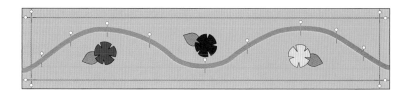

4. Sew a border strip to the top and bottom edges of the quilt center. Press seams away from the center.

5. Add 1 – 6-1/2" square to each end of the two remaining border strips for the cornerstones. Press the seams away from the cornerstones. Add borders to the side edges of the quilt center. Press seams away from the center.

6. Quilt center, including center block, 2", 4", 6", 4" and 6" borders, should now measure 56-1/2" square.

7. Use the desired appliqué patterns on pages 100 - 106 and the method of your choice to appliqué shapes onto the border.

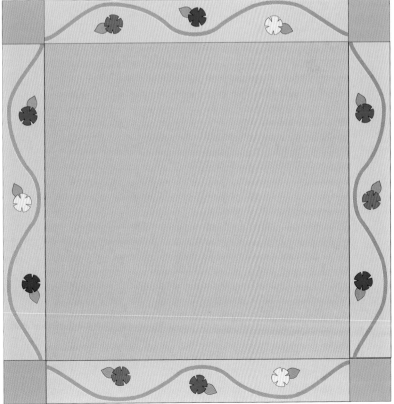

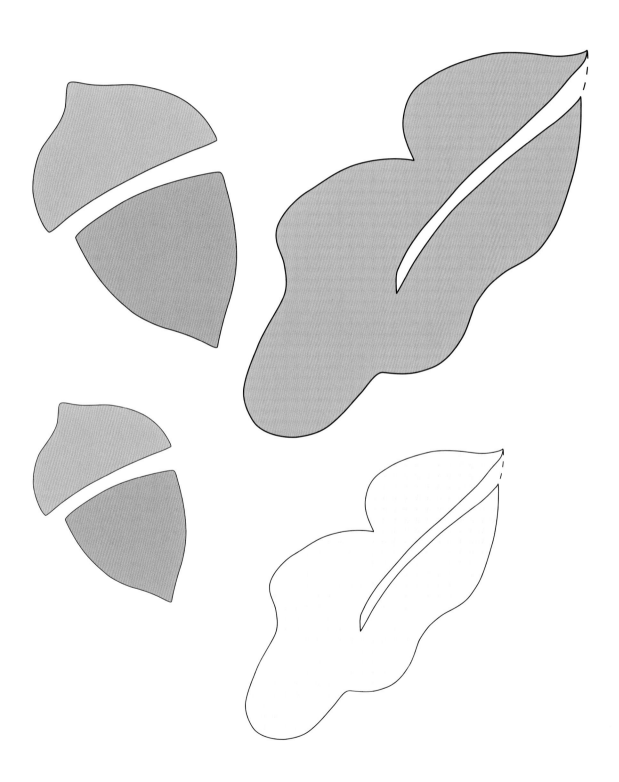

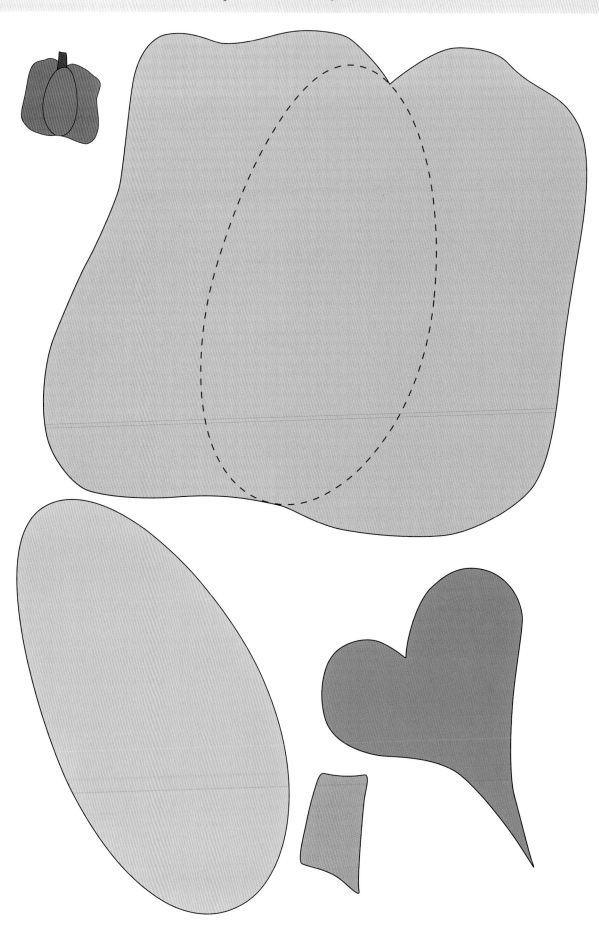

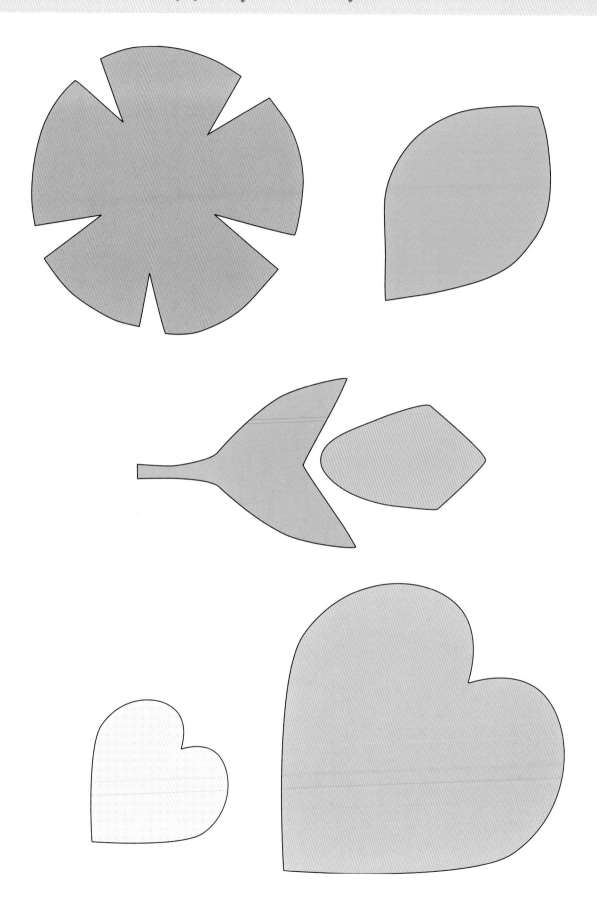

finishing the border sampler quilt

Binding is the finishing touch on your border sampler quilt. The binding covers the raw edges of the quilt center, so choose a color or fabric that complements the center's look.

A few options for binding your quilt center include:
- Pulling all the fabric used in the center of the quilt and using a bit of each for a scrappy look.
- Use a directional fabric from the center. It will add a subtle feel of movement.
- Choose a complementary binding fabric. Although it's not a fabric used in the quilt, it will pull all the colors and values together.
- Repeat the border fabric in the binding. This allows the final border to blend to the very edges of the quilt.

materials

- 3-1/2 yards of backing fabric
- 1/2 yard of binding fabric
- 62" x 62" square of batting

Cutting Instructions

From backing fabric, cut:
2—31-1/2" x 62" backing rectangles.

From binding fabric, cut:
6—2-1/2" x 42" strips.

Adding the Border

1. Sew together the 31-1/2" x 62" backing rectangles along one long edge, using a 1/2" seam allowance. Press the seam allowances open.

2. Layer the pieced backing, the batting, and the quilt center. Baste the layers together and hand-or machine-quilt as desired.

Note: *If you have not previously sewn the appliqué shapes to your border, use a buttonhole or zigzag stitch through all layers of the quilt to attach them now.*

3. Sew the 2-1/2"-wide binding strips to the edges of the quilt following the Binding instructions on page 22.

projects

Treat yourself to the fast and fun projects in this chapter. Let creativity take over and you'll be on your way to designing your own border-inspired projects.

rainbow mountains quilt

Delectable mountain blocks in a rainbow of colorful batik fabrics make up the center of this gorgeous quilt.

Finished size:
51-1/2" x 63-1/2"

Bock Size: 6"

materials

- 2-1/2 yards of dark green batik fabric
- 3-7/8" x 10" rectangle each of 13 bright batik fabrics for medium triangles
- 2-3/8" x 30" strip each of 13 bright batik fabrics for small triangles
- 2" x 42" strips from a minimum of 20 different bright batik fabrics
- 3-1/4 yards of backing fabric
- 58" x 70" square of batting

Cutting Instructions

From dark green fabric, cut:
5—6-7/8" x 42" strips.
   From the strips, cut:
   26—6-7/8"squares. Cut the squares in half diagonally to make 52 large triangles.

7—2-3/8" x 42" strips.
   From the strips, cut:
   104—2-3/8" squares. Cut the squares in half diagonally to make 208 small triangles.

8—2" x 42" strips.
   From the strips, cut:
   52—2" squares
   2—2" x 36-1/2" top and bottom inner border strips; reserve extra for side border strips.
6—2-1/2" x 42" binding strips.

From each 3-7/8" x 10" strip, cut:
2—3-7/8" squares. Cut the squares in half diagonally to make 4 medium triangles.

From each 2-3/8" x 30" strip, cut:
12—2-3/8" squares. Cut the squares in half diagonally to make 24 small triangles.

From 2" x 42" strips, cut:
120—2" x 6-1/2" rectangles.

From backing fabric, cut:
2—35-1/2" x 58" backing rectangles.

Assembling the Blocks

1. Join 1 dark green small triangle and 1 bright small triangle to make a triangle-square. Press seam toward the dark triangle. Repeat to make 4 matching triangle-squares.

Make 4

2. Sew together 2 triangle-squares and 1 matching bright small triangle as shown for Unit A.

Unit A

3. Sew together 2 triangle-squares, 1 matching bright small triangle, and 1 dark green 2" square as shown for Unit B.

Unit B

4. Arrange Unit A, Unit B, 1 bright medium triangle, and 1 dark green large triangle as shown. Join Unit A to the medium triangle; press seam toward triangle. Join Unit B; press seam toward triangle. Add the dark green large triangle to complete the block. Press seam toward large triangle. Block should measure 6-1/2" square. Repeat Steps 1-4 to make 13 sets of 4 identical blocks for a total of 52 blocks.

Make 13 sets of 4 identical blocks

Assembling the Quilt Center

1. Set aside 4 matching blocks for the outer border block cornerstones. Lay out the remaining 48 blocks on a large flat surface, taking care to position the blocks in the direction shown.

2. Sew the blocks together into rows. Press the seams of each row to one side, alternating the direction with each row. Sew the rows together to complete the quilt center. Press the seams in one direction.

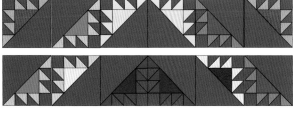

Adding the Borders

1. Sew the dark green 2" x 36-1/2" inner border strips to the top and bottom edges of the quilt center. Press seams toward the border.

2. Sew the remaining dark green 2"-wide border strips together to make one long strip. From the strip, cut 2—2" x 51-1/2" strips. Sew these to the left and right edges of the quilt center. Press seams toward the border.

3. Join 26 – 2" x 6-1/2" rectangles to make top outer border strip. Press seams in one direction. Repeat for bottom border strip.

Make 2

4. Add the pieced top and bottom outer border strips to the quilt center as shown. Press seams toward the outer border.

5. Sew together the remaining 2" x 6-1/2" rectangles in sets of 34 to make 2 side outer border strips. Press seams in one direction.

Make 2

6. Add a block cornerstone to each end of the 2 pieced side outer border strips in the direction shown. Press the seams away from the blocks. Add borders to the side edges of the quilt center. Press seams toward the outer border.

Finishing the Quilt

1. Sew together the 35-1/2" x 58" backing rectangles along one long edge, using a 1/2" seam allowance. Press the seams open.

2. Layer the pieced backing, the batting, and the quilt top. Baste the layers together and hand- or machine-quilt as desired.

3. Sew the dark green 2-1/2"-wide binding strips to the edges of the quilt following the Binding instructions on page 22.

prickly path table runner

Two rows of triangle-squares running in opposite directions make this runner an easy, quick-to-complete practice project.

Finished size:
18-1/2" x 40-1/2"

materials

- 1/3 yard of dark fabric for sawtooth triangle-squares
- 1/4 yard of light fabric for background
- 3/4 yard of print fabric for border and binding
- 22" x 44" piece of backing fabric and batting

Quilter's ruler and rotary cutter

Cutting Instructions

From dark fabric, cut:
2—2-7/8" x 42" strips.
   From the strips, cut: 28—2-7/8" squares. Cut the squares in half diagonally to make 56 triangles.
2—2-1/2" x 42" strips.
   From the strips, cut:
   2—2-1/2" x 28-1/2" strips.

From light fabric, cut:
2—2-7/8" x 42" strips.
   From the strips, cut:
   28—2-7/8" squares. Cut the squares in half diagonally to make 56 triangles.
1—2-1/2" x 42" strip.
   From the strip, cut:
   1—2-1/2" x 28-1/2" strips.

From print fabric, cut:
5—2-1/2" x 42" strips.
   From the strips, cut:
   2—2-1/2" x 28-1/2" border strips; reserve extra for binding.
1—6-1/2" x 42" strip.
   From the strip, cut:
   2—6-1/2" x 18-1/2" border rectangles.

Assembling the Table Runner

1. Join 1 light triangle and 1 dark triangle to make a triangle-square. Press seam toward the dark triangle. Repeat to make 56 triangle-squares.

Make 56

2. Sew the triangle-squares together in sets of 14 to make 2 rows as shown.

Make 2

3. Sew together the remaining triangle-squares in sets of 14 to make 2 rows as shown.

Make 2

4. Sew the rows together in pairs with a dark 2-1/2" x 28-1/2" strip; press the seams toward the strips.

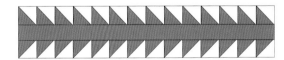

5. Sew together the pairs with the light 2-1/2" x 28-1/2" strip, pointing them in the same or opposite direction as desired.

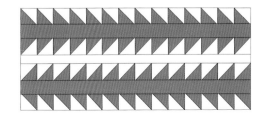

6. Sew the print 2-1/2" x 28-1/2" border strips to the long edges of the runner. Press seams toward the border.

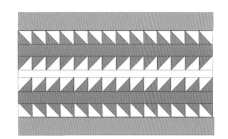

7. Sew a 6-1/2" x 18-1/2" border rectangle to each short edge of the runner. Press seams toward the rectangle.

8. Working on the wrong side of the runner, make marks along each edge, 4" away from a corner. Use a pencil to lightly draw a line connecting the marks. Cut on the pencil line. Repeat at each corner.

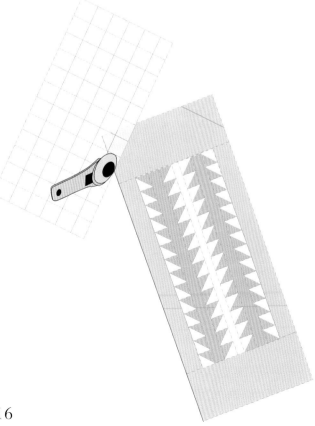

Finishing the Table Runner

1. Layer the backing, the batting, and the table runner top. Baste the layers together and hand- or machine-quilt as desired.

2. Sew the print 2-1/2"-wide binding strips to the edges of the table runner following the Binding instructions on page 22.

prickly path table runner color option

To give your table runner a different look, sew all the triangle-squares in identical directional rows.

christmas ring table runner

Alternating diamond units create a zigzag pattern on a Christmas-themed table runner.

Finished size:
19-1/2" x 44-1/2"

materials

- 1/2 yard of dark fabric for diamonds
- 1/2 yard of light fabric for background
- 1 yard of print fabric for border and binding
- 23" x 48" piece of backing fabric and batting

Quilter's ruler and rotary cutter

Cutting Instructions

From dark fabric, cut:
2—6-1/2" x 42" strips.
　From the strips, cut:
　16—3-1/2" x 6-1/2" rectangles.

From light fabric, cut:
3—3-1/2" x 42" strips.
　From the strips, cut:
　32 – 3-1/2" squares.
3—1-1/2" x 42" strips.
　From the strips, cut:
　3—1-1/2" x 24-1/2" strips.
　2—1-1/2" x 15-1/2" strips.

From print fabric, cut:
5—2-1/2" x 42" strips.
　From the strips, cut:
　2—2-1/2" x 26-1/2" border
　strips; reserve extra for binding.
1—14-1/2" square; cut the square
　in half diagonally to make 2
　border triangles.

Assembling the Table Runner

1. Draw a diagonal line on the wrong side of the light 3-1/2" squares.

2. With right sides together, align a 3-1/2" square with one end of a dark 3-1/2" x 6-1/2" rectangle as shown. Sew on the drawn line and trim the seam to 1/4". Press seams toward the small triangle.

3. Sew a second 3-1/2" square to the opposite end of the rectangle in the same manner to make a diamond unit as shown. Repeat to make 8 diamond units.

Make 8

4. Repeat Steps 2-3 to make 8 mirror-image diamond units as shown.

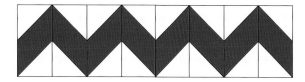

Make 8

5. Sew together and alternate 8 diamond units and 8 mirror-image diamond units as shown to make 2 rows of 8 units.

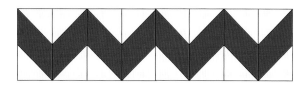

6. Add the light 1-1/2" x 24-1/2" strips to the rows as shown. Press the seams toward the strips.

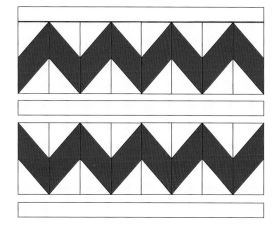

7. Sew a light 1-1/2" x 15-1/2" strip to each short edge of the runner. Press the seams toward the strips.

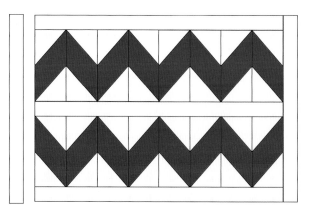

8. Sew the print 2-1/2" x 26-1/2" border strips to the long edges of the runner. Press seams toward the border.

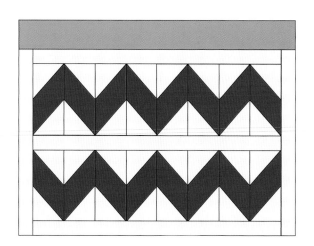

9. Center the long edge of a print border triangle on a short edge of the runner. The triangle is oversized and will extend beyond the long edges of the runner. Sew the triangle to the runner; press seams toward the triangle. Repeat with second triangle at opposite edge of runner.

Finishing the Table Runner

1. Layer the backing, the batting, and the table runner top. Baste the layers together and hand- or machine-quilt as desired.

2. Sew the print 2-1/2"-wide binding strips to the edges of the table runner following the Binding instructions on page 22.

10. To trim the oversized triangles, align the quilter's ruler with the outermost point of a triangle and an outside corner of the print border. Trim the excess from the triangle with a rotary cutter. Repeat for each raw edge of the triangles.

diamonds-in-a-row table runner

Grab three fun colors from your fabric stash and stich up this runner in a few hours. For a more scrappy look, choose a variety of fabrics for the diamonds.

Finished size:
19-1/2" x 44-1/2"

materials

- 1/2 yard of dark fabric for diamonds

- 1/2 yard of medium fabric for background

- 1 yard of print fabric for border and binding

- 23" x 48" piece of backing fabric and batting

Quilter's ruler and rotary cutter

Cutting Instructions

From dark fabric, cut:
2 – 6-1/2" x 42" strips.
  From the strips, cut:
  16 – 3-1/2" x 6-1/2" rectangles.

From medium fabric, cut:
3 – 3-1/2" x 42" strips.
  From the strips, cut:
  32 – 3-1/2" squares.
3 – 1-1/2" x 42" strips.
  From the strips, cut:
  3 – 1-1/2" x 24-1/2" strips.
  2 – 1-1/2" x 15-1/2" strips.

From print fabric, cut:
5 – 2-1/2" x 42" strips.
  From the strips, cut:
  2 – 2-1/2" x 26-1/2" border strips;
  reserve extra for binding.
1 – 14-1/2" square. Cut the square in half diagonally to make 2 border triangles.

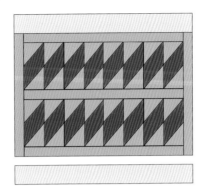

Assembling the Table Runner

1. Draw a diagonal line on the wrong side of the medium 3-1/2" squares.

2. With right sides together, align a 3-1/2" square with one end of a dark 3-1/2" x 6-1/2" rectangle as shown. Sew on the drawn line and trim the seam to 1/4". Press seams toward the small triangle.

3. Sew a second 3-1/2" square to the opposite end of the rectangle in the same manner to make a diamond unit as shown. Repeat to make 16 diamond units.

Make 16

4. Sew together 16 diamond units in sets of 8 to make 2 rows.

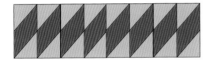

Make 2

5. Add the medium 1-1/2" x 24-1/2" strips to the rows as shown. Press the seams toward the strips.

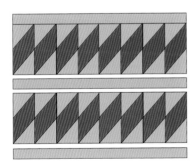

6. Sew a medium 1-1/2" x 15-1/2" strip to each short edge of the runner. Press the seams toward the strips.

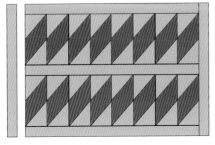

7. Sew the print 2-1/2" x 26-1/2" border strips to the long edges of the runner. Press seams toward the border.

8. Center the long edge of a print border triangle on a short edge of the runner. The triangle is oversized and will extend beyond the long edges of the runner. Sew the triangle to the runner; press seams toward the triangle. Repeat with second triangle at opposite edge of runner.

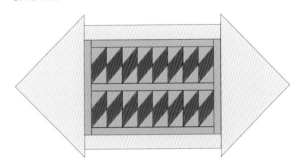

9. To trim the oversized triangles, align the quilter's ruler with the outermost point of a triangle and an outside corner of the print border. Trim the excess from the triangle with a rotary cutter. Repeat for each raw edge of the triangles.

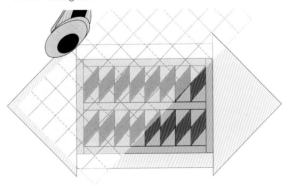

Finishing the Table Runner

1. Layer the backing, the batting, and the table runner top. Baste the layers together and hand- or machine-quilt as desired.

2. Sew the print 2-1/2"-wide binding strips to the edges of the table runner following the Binding instructions on page 22.

pick a posy table runner

Appliquéd posies adorned with leaves surround a vine in the center of this table runner.

Finished size:
14-1/2" x 38-1/2"

materials

- 1/4 yard of light fabric for background
- 1/3 yard of dark print fabric for border
- 3/4 yard of tone-on-tone fabric for cornerstones and binding
- 1-1/2"-wide dark bias strips to total 1-1/2 yards for vine
- Assorted fabric scraps for appliqué
- Plate or bowl
- 18" x 42" piece of backing fabric and batting

Cutting Instructions

From light fabric, cut:
1—6-1/2" x 30-1/2" background rectangle.

From dark print fabric, cut:
2—4-1/2" x 42" strips.
 From the strips, cut:
 2 – 4-1/2" x 30-1/2" border strips.
 2 – 4-1/2" x 6-1/2" border strips.

From tone-on-tone fabric, cut:
1—4-1/2" x 42" strip.
 From the strip, cut:
 4—4-1/2" cornerstone squares.
2-1/2"-wide bias strips to total 3-3/4 yards.

Appliqué the Table Runner

1. Sew together the 1-1/2"-wide bias strips to make one long vine strip; press the seams open. Handle bias strip gently to retain the stretch for placement on background. With wrong sides together, finger-press 1/3 of the width up. Fold remaining fabric over the first edge, folding the strip in thirds. Press.

2. Fold the 6-1/2" x 30-1/2" background rectangle in half, aligning the short edges. Fold strip in half again in the same direction. Press along the fold lines, dividing the strip into quarters. Use pins to mark the background rectangle 1-1/2" from one long edge at the side edges and center fold and 1-1/2" from the opposite long edge at the two remaining fold lines as shown.

3. Position the vine strip on the marked background rectangle, beginning at the left pin, gently curving it from pin to pin, and ending at the right pin. Baste or firmly pin the vine in place. Hand- or machine-stitch the vine in place.

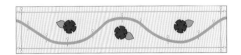

4. Use the desired patterns on pages 100 - 106 and the method of your choice to appliqué shapes onto the background referring to the diagram for placement.

Adding the Border

1. Sew the 4-1/2" x 30-1/2" dark border strip to the long edges of the background rectangle. Press seams toward the border.

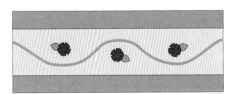

2. Add a 4-1/2" cornerstone square to each end of the 2 dark 4-1/2" x 6-1/2" border strips. Press seams away from the cornerstones. Add borders to the remaining edges of the background rectangle. Press seams toward the border.

Finishing the Table Runner

1. To round the corners, place a plate or bowl on a corner of the table runner, aligning the curve of the plate with the edges of the cornerstone. Use a pencil to lightly draw the outer curve onto the runner; cut on line. Repeat at each corner.

2. Layer the backing, the batting, and the table runner top. Baste the layers together and hand- or machine-quilt as desired. Trim through all layers on the pencil lines at the corners.

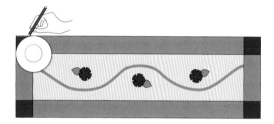

3. Sew the tone-on-tone 2-1/2"-wide binding strips to the edges of the quilt following the Binding instructions on page 22.

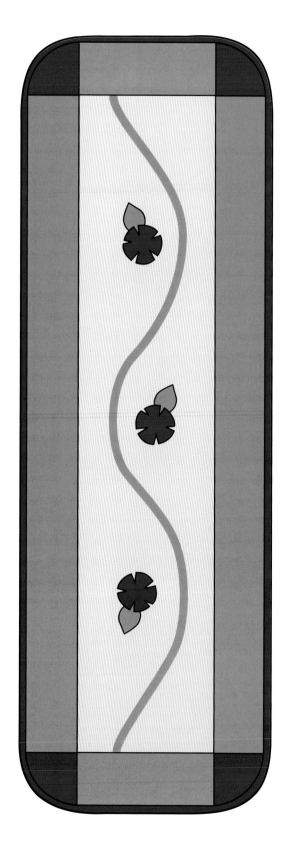

pick a posy table runner color option

Transform your table to autumn with acorns and leaves in fall-like fabrics.

thankyou

A few special Thank Yous to my family and friends
who have always supported and encouraged my quilting life.

To my husband Jim, genius of all things that can be built.

Jason, my engineering son, who is married to Army Captain Angela.

Matt, my measuring son, who is married to Dawn, mother of my first grandchild.

To my Mom, who encouraged me to sew at a young age
and went with me to my first quilting class.

To my Dad, fixer of all things, including sewing machines!

And to my quilting friends, both near and far,
you know who you are and you know you are my "real" friends!

Jill

Thank you also to:

United Notions/Moda Fabrics for supplying
many of the fabrics used in the photography and quilting projects.

The Warm™ Company for supplying Warm and Natural Batting
used in all of the quilting projects.

Presencia Threads for supplying threads used in block construction and quilting.

Creekside Quilting for the use of the Delectable Mountain Block of the Month,
the starter for my Rainbow Mountain Quilt.

Resources:

Creekside Quilting
  Connie Doern
  9926 Swanson Blvd.
  Clive, Iowa 50325
  515/276-1977
  www.creekside-quilting.com

Master Piece Products
  10481 NW 107th Ave.
  Granger, Iowa 50109
  515/999-2746
  mpquilt@aol.com

Presencia Threads
  Bag Lady Inc.
  PO Box 2409
  Evergreen, Colorado 80437-2409
  888-222-4523
  www.baglady.com

The Warm™ Company
  5529 186th Place SW
  Lynnwood, Washington 98037
  425/248-2424
  www.warmcompany.com

United Notions/Moda Fabrics
  www.unitednotion.com